Leadership
Therapy

Leadership Therapy

Inside the Mind of Microsoft

Anna Rowley, Ph.D.

palgrave
macmillan

First published in 2007 by
PALGRAVE MACMILLAN™
175 Fifth Avenue, New York, N.Y. 10010 and
Houndmills, Basingstoke, Hampshire, England RG21 6XS
Companies and representatives throughout the world.

PALGRAVE MACMILLAN is the global academic imprint of the Palgrave Macmillan division of St. Martin's Press, LLC and of Palgrave Macmillan Ltd. Macmillan® is a registered trademark in the United States, United Kingdom and other countries. Palgrave is a registered trademark in the European Union and other countries.

ISBN-13: 978–1–4039–8403–6
ISBN-10: 1–4039–8403–4

Library of Congress Cataloging-in-Publication Data

Rowley, Anna.
    Leadership therapy: inside the mind of Microsoft / Anna Rowley.
      p. cm.
    Includes bibliographical references and index.
    ISBN 1–4039–8403–4
      1. Leadership. 2. Success in business. 3. Executive ability. I. Title.

HD57.7.R69 2007
658.4′092—dc22
                                               2007016213

A catalogue record for this book is available from the British Library.

Design by Newgen Imaging Systems (P) Ltd., Chennai, India.

First edition: December 2007

10 9 8 7 6 5 4 3 2 1

Printed in the United States of America.

This book is dedicated to Stan and Dorothy,
my parents, who always believed.

Contents

Contents

Preface and Acknowledgments

I first started writing this book in Paris, France, and finished it on a train from Agra to New Delhi in India. For the past 14 years this has been my life, traveling the globe working as a psychologist and therapist to some of the most driven, achievement-oriented and often most complex people on the planet—the leaders who work for the technology giant Microsoft. It seems hard to believe that 25 years ago Microsoft was a small startup with just a handful of employees when its workforce now numbers in the tens of thousands. It's also hard to think of a time when their products weren't ubiquitous—love them or hate them, Microsoft changed the way many in the world communicate and work together. What is less well known are the struggles of the people behind these technological advances—the same struggles many of us face in our work—insecurity, insufficient trust, frustrated ambition, burnout, and a lack of belief either in ourselves, or others, or the work we do. *Leadership Therapy* is the true stories of the leaders I have worked with—from Windows '95 to Vista—and it is the true stories of how they overcame these barriers to achieve career success that are at the heart of this book.

One of my most closely held beliefs, one I share with many of the leaders I work with, is that you can't be successful on your own, and achievement is an effort. I want to take this opportunity to acknowledge the help and support I have had on my own journey in bringing this book from an idea to the one you hold in your hands.

First and foremost I'd like to thank Stephanie Land, my editor, who worked with me on every step of the writing process. Writing can be a lonely pursuit but Stephanie made it a shared project and I thank her for her insight and intelligence. A big debt of gratitude goes to Airié Stuart, my publisher, who was willing to bet on me and an idea, and who has been one of my biggest supporters. I also want to thank Lorin Rees, my agent, for his support from the very beginning. I must also thank some very special people in Microsoft. Simon Witts has been a champion of my work from the very beginning and his feedback on an early draft of the book was invaluable. Leslie Osborne also cast a critical eye over the text and suggested some important improvements. Others who gave freely of their time were Matt Lindenburg, Elissa Murphy, Rajiv Kumar, and in particular Mark Hill who took me on a tour of his childhood with no stone left unturned. Others who championed the effort and were part of my virtual team were Dave Hinton, Andrew Hawken, and Mary Crothers. I also want to thank Barb Gordon for her stories and support, and Blake Irving for building the best team I have ever worked with. I also want to thank Professor Philip Graham—my first and most important mentor.

Finally I must thank my family, who sacrificed the most over the eight months when I was writing *Leadership Therapy* and going through the emotional highs and lows that often accompany an endeavor like this. To Cyd, Jamie, Corey, and Zoey much love; I couldn't have done this without you.

Leadership
Therapy

Introduction

"So, tell me about your childhood." This may seem an odd question to ask a manager—any employee, really—within the confines of company walls. But it's a commonplace one at Microsoft. Not that people walk around carrying boxes of Kleenex and confessing their innermost thoughts to their cube mates. Yet it is often one of the first things I ask when I walk into my clients' offices.

I'm not your typical therapist. I don't run a private practice catering to a wide range of patients struggling with eating disorders or ruined marriages or agoraphobia. In fact, my patients are some of the most successful, powerful, put-together, take-charge people in the corporate world. So what are they doing in therapy? And why are we having our sessions right in the middle of the workday, at the office?

Cultivating leadership is of the utmost importance at Microsoft. A lot of companies talk a good game, but Microsoft's investment in its leadership talent does not end with the "welcome to the team" handshake. From their very first day, employees at Microsoft are encouraged to do whatever it takes to become more effective and successful. For some, that means a visit with the company therapist.

A MAP OF THE PSYCHE

Fourteen years ago, Microsoft brought me on board as a consulting psychologist to help executive teams and individuals throughout the company maximize their potential. I have met with hundreds of ambitious leaders at all ranks within the company, every one of them committed to becoming the best they can be. We leave no stone unturned in that mission, tackling the traditional blockades to professional advancement, such as inadequate or deficient communication skills, problems "managing up" to the boss or dealing with conflict or confrontation, but we also delve into complex psychological questions that address why these issues might have come up in the first place—thus, my ubiquitous question about a client's childhood.

By the time I see most of my clients, they have hit a wall. They're overachievers used to a rapid ascent up the corporate ladder who suddenly find themselves struggling to keep their momentum, arguing with teammates, or plagued by insecurity. Once they recognize they have a problem, they'll do whatever they can to stop sabotaging, inhibiting, or undermining their effectiveness, and, ultimately, their careers. My job is to help them figure out what's wrong, and then create a map—of the psyche, if you will—that allows them to acknowledge, confront, and work through the hidden psychological and emotional minefields that are hindering their progress.

In the fourteen years that I've worked at Microsoft, I've discovered that regardless of why someone comes to see me—whether they are struggling with communicating the strategic direction of their business or dealing with an overaggressive subordinate—ultimately the root of their problem comes down to a struggle with one (and sometimes more than one) of five universal issues:

1. Belief
2. Self-Awareness
3. Self-Confidence

4. Trust
5. Power

What do you believe in? How do you see yourself? How do you impact others? Are you decisive—yes, no, or maybe? What do you think you deserve? Does approval motivate your behavior? Does success define your self-worth? When is it hard for you to trust? These questions cut across age, gender, role, and geography. Whether you work for big business or a mom-and-pop shop, whether you're a CEO, teacher, or professional landscape artist, the answers to these questions will directly impact whether you attain the heights of your ambitions or eventually find yourself banging on closed doors.

I wrote *Leadership Therapy* to help prop open those doors for anyone who knows that there is more they want to achieve in their careers but feel stymied by forces they're not sure they can identify, much less control. People often think they are alone in dealing with these problems, but I have found that these psychological brick walls are the same in Toronto as they are in Madrid or Hyderabad, India.

I've worked with countless clients, from Olympic hopefuls to hardened business types, and the methodology outlined in these pages can help any leader break down the obstacles we all inadvertently place in the way of our professional success. I've been privileged by how forthcoming my clients have been about sharing the details of their lives. It is because of them that I've been able to pinpoint the essential truths and universal challenges people face as they struggle to create a fulfilling work life and self.

There is a catch, of course. You have to *want* to change. Just as I can't help anyone who isn't prepared to do the deep mental excavation required for successful therapeutic breakthroughs, this book is only for people who have the passion, commitment, and courage to take a hard look at their lives and identify what they have to do differently. It's for people interested in going beyond the superficial and rediscovering what makes them tick, what motivates them to do what they do. Some people find this process fascinating, and others find it exceedingly uncomfortable. But the effort is worth the tremendous rewards.

SHORT TERM CORPORATE THERAPY

Leadership Therapy will reveal the workings of Short Term Corporate Therapy, the therapeutic system I created to address the needs and time constraints of people eager to improve their leadership skills and job performance. As a result of this approach, my clients are able to:

- Identify the core beliefs that drive their behavior and subsequently employ them to motivate and inspire their teams;
- boost their self-acceptance, which lowers their levels of stress and job dissatisfaction;
- increase their tolerance for ambiguity and change;
- make better decisions about the people they work with—who to hire, who to promote, and who to trust;
- accurately predict the behavior of others so that they can manage up, across, and down with maximum impact and influence;
- acknowledge that behaviors that have helped them succeed previously may now be inhibiting their future achievements;
- improve their self-awareness, one of the most significant sources of power and a direct influence on one's success; and
- build businesses that motivates their people to get out of bed in the morning rather than keep them awake at night.

With a solid grasp of the therapeutic rationale grounding each step of the process, readers will be able to participate in a self-directed version of the same analytical process I offer my clients.

Short Term Corporate Therapy is not a watered-down version of psychotherapy aimed at the time-starved denizens of modern corporations. The underpinnings of my methodology are rooted in the same rigorously tested and proven tenets of Short Term Psychotherapy used by any traditional therapist. The major difference between my approach and traditional psychotherapy is location. Thanks to recent advances in the therapeutic process, which I discuss further in chapter 1, I'm no longer dependent on what my client chooses to tell me in a 50-minute session in my office. I follow my clients into the workplace, which allows me an unprecedented opportunity to watch them in action, to observe not only how they react, but how their colleagues react to them. I can compare what they think is happening to what is actually happening (the discrepancy is often tremendous). This fly-on-the-wall perspective gives me a huge advantage over psychiatrists, psychologists, and therapists who rely on the traditional therapeutic model.

While not a self-help guide, this book should provide you with enough insight to conduct your own version of Short Term Corporate Therapy, allowing you to look at your own workplace environment and behavior with fresh eyes, to take stock of what's working and what's not. You'll be forced to take a hard look at what drives you to make the choices that have led you to this point. The pressure to perform, the financial stakes, even our commute times—all of it is increasing, and fast. Most of us can't control these elements of the twenty-first century work world, but we can control how we feel about it. We can control how we decide to cope with it. We can control whether we allow our past to dictate our present and our future. We can control how we handle the unexpected surprises life hands us.

Although many of the theories you'll read about were developed and tested at Microsoft, this isn't a book about Microsoft, nor is it strictly for the tech set or people at the upper echelons of their fields. Microsoft simply provided the perfect petri dish for me to study the challenges leaders face when working in intense environments. Microsoft's leaders swim in some of the most competitive, fast-moving waters around. Many survive on very little sleep, face ridiculously short turn-around times, and find their teams in constant flux. In this company, only the strong survive. So it's safe to say that if my methods can empower people working in this type of "extreme" environment, they can empower anyone.

THE STRAIGHTEST ROAD TO SUCCESS

While there have been books about personality types, emotional intelligence, and even intuition, this book explores uncharted terrain of corporate performance: the psyche. *Leadership Therapy* unveils the common themes, issues, and challenges I have witnessed working intimately with leaders at the highest levels to achieve a deeper understanding of who they are and who they want to become. As you will learn from my stories about the men and women who have bravely and candidly shared with me their hopes, dreams, and fears, the straightest road to success is not begun by rolling up our sleeves and blindly forging ahead, but by sitting down to take stock of the past, the present, and the future we desire.

1

From Couch to Corporate

The Origins of Short Term Corporate Therapy

I am often asked to describe the theoretical underpinnings of my work. Am I a Freudian, a cognitive psychologist, or a positive psychologist? The answers I give are invariably yes, yes, and yes. Like many therapists practicing today I am eclectic in my approach and let the needs of the client dictate my method. Certain practitioners and theoreticians have had a tremendous impact on the development of Short Term Corporate Therapy (STCT). For newcomers to this type of therapy, being aware of the roots of my practice is key to understanding what it is—and what it isn't—and helps pave the way for the work that lies ahead.

FROM COUCH TO CORPORATE

The origins of psychotherapy—the "talking cure"—can be traced back to a small suite of rooms at 19 Berggasse in Vienna, Austria. It was here that Sigmund Freud saw his most famous patients—the Rat Man, the Wolf Man, Little Hans and Dora—and developed his theories of the unconscious, the ego, the id and super ego, Freudian slips, and dream symbolism. His work changed the way mental health professionals and society at large understood the working of the mind. His famous couch became synonymous with Freudian theory and practice and has become an iconic representation of psychoanalysis.[1] However, over the past one hundred years the process of psychotherapy has changed significantly. Market forces dictated that the open-ended approach, where patients could spend years in analysis, be supplemented where appropriate by more pragmatic, focused, time-limited methods, and therapists were urged to find a more efficient way of managing a patient's mental health and well-being.

The breakthrough occurred in the 1960s in Pennsylvania, where a psychiatrist named Aaron T. Beck developed the next revolution in mental health, one that has become the treatment of choice for many psychotherapists around the world. To put the scale of Beck's transformation in context, it was akin to going from Henry T. Ford's "any color Model T as long as it's black" to the array of colors and finishes we can choose for our vehicles today. Beck suggested that rather than spend time analyzing the unconscious mind, a process that can take many years, a more pragmatic approach would be to focus instead on conscious, internal communications—analyzing a patient's thoughts and feelings. In particular, he argued that the key to understanding why we do what we do, and why we feel the way we feel, lay in the "automatic thoughts" that run through our minds as we experience things; the assumptions and rules that guide our behavior; and the beliefs we hold about ourselves, others and the world around us. These patterns of cognition can be like sleeper cells, lying dormant until they are activated by a specific experience or event, or they can become a permanent way of perceiving the world.

One of my earliest clients offers an excellent demonstration of how our beliefs, thoughts, and assumptions can undermine our leadership capabilities. Bob wanted me to help him establish his personal brand. He had worked for several high-profile executives in the company and wanted to position himself as a leader in his own right, not just someone who got things done for others. On the surface it seemed like a fairly straightforward request. Bob seemed to be a confident, powerful, and committed leader. Finding his unique selling points wouldn't be difficult—or so it seemed. I shadowed Bob, observing his behavior during various meetings and during an important strategy session with his leadership team. I noted that when Bob talked to his team he often relied on self-canceling messages—contradictory or invalidating statements. For example he would say, "This is what I think we should do, but it's only my opinion," or, "I'm passionate about this, but you may have a better idea." These statements were confusing and frustrating to his team, and they were dampening his power and effectiveness.

Over the course of a few sessions, Bob revealed a negative core belief: Asserting his convictions would create unnecessary conflict. He was comfortable communicating other people's ideas and directives, but he faltered when communicating his own, protecting himself by either attributing them to someone else or using self-canceling messages. When he found himself in front of his team, his automatic thoughts sounded something like this: "If I push these ideas and people don't like them I'm going to look really stupid," and, "It's safer to spread responsibility for these ideas by offering them as suggestions." I asked Bob to think about where his beliefs and behaviors came from. During a later session he revealed excitedly, "I know why I do this! My mom was the driver in the family. She was smarter than my dad and often came up with the best ideas. To avoid antagonizing my dad she 'softened' her opinions by adding things like, 'But that's just me. You probably have a much better idea.' I think I inherited [the tendency toward self-canceling messages] from her." By becoming aware of how his patterns of negative thinking caused conflict rather than avoided it, Bob (with a little help from me) was able to modify his beliefs and assumptions so that he could take ownership of his ideas and be unafraid to voice his opinions.

Short Term Corporate Therapy works because it doesn't let us off the hook. It doesn't allow us to waste time fishing around for people or circumstances to blame for our problems. As one of my clients once blurted out, "It's not the job—it's me!" (We'll see in chapter 2 how acknowledging our experiences can be a force for significant growth and self-actualization.) Not only does STCT enable me to help clients like Bob in an efficient and effective manner, but I can do so anywhere, at any time, face-to-face, on the telephone, or by e-mail. My practice, much like the twenty-first century workplace, knows no boundaries.

PSYCHOTHERAPY AND THE WORKPLACE

The days when sunrise meant you got up for work and sunset marked the end of the day are long gone.[2] The natural rhythms of life have been suspended and business is conducted 24/7. Reports of job stress, with its associated symptoms of cynicism and emotional exhaustion, are on the rise thanks to the debilitating need for speed in the always-on world of business. We're also seeing more absenteeism (an increase in the number of overall sick days and reports of depression and burnout) and presenteesim (low performance while at work). An increasing number of employees worldwide are reporting emotional problems such as insomnia and depression, as well as stress-related physical ailments such as hypertension and increased susceptibility to illness and disease.[3]

I have worked with many people who refuse to take vacations fearing the mountain of e-mail that will greet them on their return to work. The organization now reaches far beyond the bricks-and-mortar of the office building. People's boundaries are bombarded by digital demands and many feel powerless to prevent it.

Yet STCT is based on the understanding that our mental health hinges on much more than freedom from job stress. It depends upon our capacity for: (a) what Abraham Maslow called self-actualization—the ability of a person to fully exploit their talents, capabilities, and potential; (b) subjective well-being—the experience of happiness and exuberance; and (c) resilience—the ability to rebound from stress or adversity, to be steeled, not scarred by adverse experience. Short Term Corporate Therapy is designed to:

- help leaders overcome self-imposed psychological barriers, actualize their potential, and maximize their impact on the business;
- boost self-esteem, feelings of well-being, confidence, and optimism;
- promote resilience as a core skill so that a leader can feel comfortable dealing with ambiguity, transformation and change; and
- equip leaders with the skills to be become their own coach/therapist.

FOUNDATIONS OF STCT

The journey that led to the development of the STCT model started during my undergraduate studies at Loughborough University in

England, and became fully formed at the Institute of Child Health, London, the medical school for Great Ormond Street Hospital. Since I wrote my undergraduate thesis some thirty years ago I have gravitated to the interpersonal school of psychology. It makes sense to me that many people's problems are caused by their relationships with others. My guide to understanding the role and significance of interpersonal relationships was the work of Harry Stack Sullivan, a little-known American psychiatrist who founded the interpersonal approach to psychotherapy. Sullivan believed that psychotherapy should focus on an individual's relationships with others and the effect a person's social and cultural environment has on his or her well-being. He proposed that everything we do in our relationships is driven by a need to achieve and maintain self-esteem and avoid anxiety.[4] As the British psychiatrist John Brown noted:

> We have tended in the past to suppose we are self contained individuals looking out from a tower of our own private castle from which we proceed on periodic excursions in order to satisfy physical, emotional and mental needs and desires. We assumed that our contacts with the world left us relatively untouched, the same person as before. In the opinion of Sullivan this is a complete fallacy; we do not merely have experiences—we are our experiences.[5]

I used Sullivan's theories to drive my post-graduate research on the relationship between personality and performance in high performance sports teams. Based on this research, I was recruited to head up a study into the effects of intensive training on elite athletes at the Institute of Child Health. At the time there were many reports of young, successful athletes suffering debilitating injuries, chronic emotional problems such as depression, and abuse from parents determined to see their child win. Ours was the first study of its kind in the world, and my job was to design the program and manage a multi-disciplinary team following several cohorts of young athletes over several years. It was a particularly exciting time to be at the Institute, which was at the cutting edge of therapeutic models, a destination spot where therapists engaged in groundbreaking research and could speak to the new generation of practitioners. It was here that I was introduced to the two additional theorists who would most influence my practice and play an enormous part in the development of Short Term Corporate Therapy.

ON THE SHOULDERS OF GIANTS

During the early design stages of the young athlete study, a chance encounter with a colleague completely changed the way I thought about health and illness and the purpose of our research. Most Monday mornings at the Institute I'd talk with the other clinicians and researchers. We'd catch up with the progress of each other's work before heading off to meet clients, patients, or research subjects. One morning a fellow psychologist was discussing her weekend at a conference in Ireland. She talked about a presentation by a Professor Garmezy, and the impact his research into resilience had had upon her thinking about family systems and child health.

Norman Garmezy was well known. He and others in the field of resilience research turned the focus of psychology and psychopathology on its head. Why, he argued, do we continue to concentrate on illness and disease when we can learn so much from people who survive, and sometimes thrive, in environments of danger, deprivation, or adversity?[6] Over the past thirty years resilience research has had a tremendous impact on our understanding of health and provided many significant insights into how children, families, and even organizations can become resilient and cope more effectively with change or adversity.

Subsequent discussions with my colleague and further investigation into Garmezy's work prompted me to think differently about my own research. What if, instead of following the conventional route and looking for rates of pathology and ill health on young athletes in training, we looked at how the intense resilience of young people engaged in performance extremes could raise self-confidence and self-esteem, and protect them from emotional problems? It seemed an exciting opportunity to break new ground. The Training of Young Athletes Study, or TOYA as it became known, would enable us to analyze whether young people engaging in performance extremes (training and competition) were resilient or could acquire resilience. Not only had I discovered a fresh way of looking at the problem of dysfunction in young athletes, I had discovered the first pillar of what would become STCT.

The second and final pillar came from the work of an ebullient family therapist named Salvador Minuchin. Heralded as a genius for his groundbreaking way of looking at the power dynamics of a family, Minuchin and his theory of Structural Family Therapy[7] provided a way to understand some basic truths about my young athletes, as well as a framework for my work with leaders in Microsoft. I often ask teams this question: "If this team were a family, what would it be like?" The answers give me huge insight into the structural dynamics of team relationships.

Minuchin discovered two problems common to troubled families. Some families are "enmeshed"—disordered and tightly interconnected.

Others are "disengaged," meaning family relationships are fragmented.[8] In both, families lack clear lines of authority. Enmeshed parents are too intertwined with their children to exercise leadership and control, disengaged parents too remote to provide support and guidance. At the time, anecdotal evidence presupposed that the parents of young athletes were enmeshed—overly involved in their children's sport, bullying, cajoling, and threatening the young athlete to succeed. By studying the family dynamics both in the young athletes' homes, as well as at the Institute, we dispelled this myth. Over three years, we found these families to be far from troubled. Instead they were cohesive, adaptable, and supportive with strong leadership exercised by the parents. One of the main findings that emerged from the study was that the families of young athletes didn't cause emotional or behavior problems in these young children. Rather, the families were the main force protecting their children. Such was the strength of this finding that we went so far as to recommend that so-called normal families whose children did not take part in high-level sport should adopt some of the characteristics from these "super families."

Within my practice at Microsoft I have used Minuchin's theories when counseling leaders and their teams. For example, one of my clients, Mike, was referred to me after relations between him and his new team completely broke down. Mike had recently joined the company and was eager to make his mark. However, he had replaced a very charismatic leader who had kept the team together through the sheer force of his personality. After talking to Mike and members of his team it was clear that Mike had to learn what I call the boundary tango. I often see this dance played out in large meetings or social gatherings. One person, let's call him Steve, moves to talk to Brian. Steve isn't aware of how his presence is affecting Brian and as he moves closer,

Brian steps back. Steve moves in to close the gap and Brian once again moves to maintain distance between them. This boundary tango continues until Brian is rescued by a friend or colleague, Steve moves away to dance with someone else, or Brian stands his ground and tells Steve to back off. Mike, like Steve in the example, wasn't giving his team any room to move on their own. The more he pushed the team to accept his authority the more they resisted and moved back. The more they resisted the more frustrated he became. He started to behave like an overinvolved, overinvested parent, asking and then answering his own questions, insisting on having the last word, going into what the team called broadcast mode—telling them what to do rather than listening to differing points of view. By joining the team for a day, much as Minuchin infiltrated the homes of the families he studied, I was able to "out" these dysfunctional ways of communicating and restore trust between Mike and his team so that their dance became more of a give and take, rather than a push and pull.

INTO THE WORKPLACE

Over the course of my twelve years at the Institute, my team followed over five hundred young athletes between the ages of eight and twenty, each for over three years. Some of these children went on to participate in the Olympics. Some became professional tennis players, while others joined professional soccer clubs. We found that this population was significantly more resilient when compared to an age-matched control group who didn't take part in competitive sport. They had a significantly lower risk of depression, higher levels of self-esteem, and perceived their families to be closer and more cohesive than children from the comparison population. Further analysis indicated that children from the comparison population, children who weren't involved in intense physical training, were more than nine times more likely to have low self-esteem and high depression scores than children who were involved in high-level competitive sport. Why? What factors protected these children from the physical, emotional, and psychological effects of stress, whereas others derailed when faced with stress, turning to alcohol or drugs or other self-destructive behavior? In total we identified five protective factors that helped these children cope with the stress of participating in high-level competitive sport:

1. A close, supportive family environment characterized by mutual trust and respect.
2. High self-esteem. These athletes' deep involvement and commitment to succeeding in their sport facilitated a strong sense of self-worth. These young people felt good at something, a belief that gave them a sense of control and mastery over other experiences and events in their lives.
3. A clear sense of purpose and goals. The routine of training and competition gave these young people a sense of discipline and an ability to delay gratification. These weren't short-term goals but multi-year objectives they worked toward season after season.
4. Discipline and an unwavering focus on the goal or prize. Though sport was not the only thing in these young people's lives, they knew how to prioritize and manage the multiple demands on their time and commitment.
5. The interest and support of other people who were not their parent (in this instance the coach). The athletes were good recruiters—able to enlist the help of others who could help them in their quest.

In 1993, the surprising findings of my research team became the subject of a BBC documentary and numerous radio and newspaper reports. Then, in 1994 I was contacted by David Svendsen, then General Manager of Microsoft UK. An urbane Australian with a passion for marathon running and mountain climbing (he spent one sabbatical climbing Everest), David's participation in extreme sports inspired him to think his executive team could benefit from working with me. As it happened, I had long wanted to explore the idea of applying my research to organizations. Resilient athletes seemed to share many common traits and experiences with successful corporate leaders. Both types generally create high performance teams characterized by mutual trust and respect; they have high self-esteem and are deeply committed to winning; they have a clear sense of purpose and long-term, often multi-year goals; they have the ability to prioritize and multitask; they rely strongly on their belief in themselves; and, finally, they are unafraid of failure. It followed that if I could help athletes successfully cope with the emotional pressures of their environment, I might be able to do the same for people in business.

To begin, I translated my research findings into a methodology that would measure the resilience of David's leadership team. I developed a "Resilience Audit" to determine the ability of the team to cope with the turbulent corporate culture of Microsoft and deal with the inevitable ambiguity that working for the company involved. It was a particularly exciting time for Microsoft. The company was experiencing unprecedented growth and was readying itself for the launch of Windows '95—the killer app of the mid-1990s. But were they ready for a psychotherapist?

THE EARLY DAYS

My arrival at Microsoft was met with some trepidation. Even though the team didn't say anything, their expressions told me they were wondering what I was doing there. Why would they need a psychologist? I usually broke the ice by saying I had spent the previous ten years working in child psychology and that made me uniquely qualified to work with leaders in their company. My joke always got a laugh and I decided early on that to survive and make a difference, humor and assertion were my best allies. Microsoft was no academic ivory tower. It didn't take long for teams to respond to my edgy, confrontational approach. I explicitly asked that there be no boardroom table in any room in which I worked. I wanted people to leave behind the office mindset and interact without the barrier of a table or the distraction of e-mail or cell phones. I borrowed and developed exercises from family therapy to examine the strength and direction of relationships within a team. For example, one such exercise asks each member to chart their work relationships. They place themselves at the center of a circle, representing a room, and then position everyone else according to the strength or weakness of their relationship. The better the relationship, the closer to the center of the circle. The result is a "map" of the team's relationships. One individual was so unpopular with his colleagues that every one of them positioned him outside the room. It's hard to ignore that kind of feedback!

I also took teams on field trips. We visited with tennis pros to hear what they had to say about how their team was affected by good coaching. I had them play against Arsenal soccer team juniors so I could see how they performed under pressure. We also played basketball. It was great for morale, and I'd use the game as a jumping-off point for a discussion on appreciating the work other people did. For example, just as an individual playing offense could recognize the value of a good defense, so could a sales manager appreciate the contribution of Marketing. I also had whole departments make a movie together to foster cross-group working (I have seen some very, very dark interpretations of *The Wizard of Oz*). Over time my reputation spread and more teams wanted to work with me. Individuals, too, began asking for private sessions. I began to split my time between teamwork and face-to-face meetings.

I had considerable success working with teams. Many arrived plagued by a lack of trust, direction, and purpose, and left as a "real team,"[9] trusting each other, clear about their vision and mission and what they needed from one another to succeed. But in the one-on-ones, something was going wrong. For individual counseling, I had always favored a non-directional approach—the opposite of the in-your-face style I used with teams. I'd ask open-ended questions. I'd guide the conversation, but with a very light touch. At the end of our time together, I'd praise my client for being open and candid and would send them on their way until our next meeting. But after a few weeks, I could tell people were getting frustrated. More than once, on hearing me start to wind things down and wish them a good week, they'd look at me with a puzzled expression and ask, "That's it? What do I do now?" At first I was unconcerned. Frustration at the end of a session is often a sign that progress has been made, that the client has revealed something that has made them uncomfortable, which means it's likely they will spend the seven days until they see me again thinking about what we have talked about. My own analyst once referred to this as building up a "therapeutic head of steam." But in this case, rather than "steaming ahead" to insight and well-being, my clients seemed to be running on empty. People were questioning my "value-add" to the business and becoming disillusioned by the open-ended nature of the process. Yet I was sure I had done everything right. I'd listened attentively. I'd interpreted key behaviors. I'd asked insightful questions. What more did they want? It was their job to go away and figure their problems out for themselves. I was merely to lead them to the water; I couldn't force them to drink. Could I?

BECOMING ONE OF THEM

And then it hit me. These were natural-born problem-solvers, and they weren't about to wait a whole week before trying to fix whatever wasn't working. I quickly realized that I had underestimated what these people wanted from me. They weren't coming to me for Band-Aids; they were prepared to undergo surgery, and the sooner the better. The more traditional, analytical approach to therapy wasn't going to work. They needed me to be much more hands-on, as I was in my team meetings. They needed me to become one of them—focused, results-oriented, an agitator. They needed me to develop a program, complete with goals and benchmarks, that would allow them to actively work on what they learned during our sessions within their everyday corporate environment.

I stopped being subtle (which wasn't hard) and started to challenge, interrupt, and dispute. I started telling my clients what I thought their problem was, and what they should do about it. In this way, Short Term Corporate Therapy began to evolve.

THE PROCESS

Short Term Corporate Therapy (STCT) is unique in four ways:

1. *It is time-limited.* The first thing I learned from working in the business world is that Time is Money. In reality, I work for two masters: My client, and the company. The organization wants its employees to be working at full effectiveness as soon as possible. Just as no organization would take their employees' word for it that they are meeting their numbers, no organization is going to pay for six months in therapy and not have anything to show for it. The second thing I learned is that ambitious people—the kind who are generally drawn to working with me—thrive on a sense of urgency. Any leader who knows they are operating below their potential knows that their performance will eventually negatively affect the company's bottom line, and any leader who negatively affects the company's bottom line isn't going to last there very long. By limiting our time together to an average of twelve to twenty sessions, I force myself to come up with creative ways to ensure that my clients make progress from week to week, and my clients feel confident that they will see improvements in a relatively short time. In addition, the company is satisfied, knowing that its investment in employees will pay off in real and visible ways.

2. *It solves problems, not symptoms.* All forms of short-term psychotherapy emphasize the importance of solving the "central issue"—the real problem, as opposed to the "presenting" problem, which is usually merely a symptom of the central issue. For example, John was referred to me after being repeatedly told by peers and supervisors that he had poor listening skills. His direct reports felt he wasn't interested in what they had to say, and others in the business found him dismissive. We could have spent time working through his presenting problem—poor listening skills—by helping him restate what he heard,

promoting a greater understanding of why he listened and why he switched off, and identifying his preferred listening style. The real problem, however, wasn't John's ability to listen but his self-consciousness and anxiety. He was so focused on looking good or always having the right answer that he couldn't attend to what people were saying. Before he could learn to listen well, he would have to overcome his deep-rooted fear of failure and ridicule.

3. *It takes place in situ.* Most psychotherapeutic approaches cocoon the therapist and client together away from family, friends, or coworkers, creating an intimate, one-on-one dynamic. Yet the only way to understand my client's behavior and the impact it might have on the people they work with is to infiltrate their work environment and see where the real behavior manifests itself. To this end I've adapted Salvador Minuchin's philosophy that a therapist is like an anthropologist who must first join and be accepted by a culture before being able to study it.[10] The likelihood of people accepting my observations and interventions increases exponentially if I join their team and milieu. I follow people within their work environment and ask for feedback directly from colleagues, direct reports, and teammates. I use a range of methods: informal interviews with members of my client's team, direct observation, participating in the life of the group, conducting collective discussions, analyzing company documents that outline formal job descriptions and mandates. It's the equivalent of obtaining a family or educational history.

This shift from relying on a single point of focus—my client's perspective—to a collective focus—many perspectives, including my own—as well as taking into account a client's behavior, represents a tremendous difference between STCT and other brief psychotherapies. Yet these combined methods provide me with a richer, more comprehensive toolkit with which to diagnose and treat my clients.

4. *It offers real world practice.* One of the main problems facing any short-term therapist is how to keep up with the patient once the session is over.[11] For my work to be successful, the client has to be able to carry over the lessons learned in therapy to the real world. Yet it's here where the urgent often gets in the way of the important. The needs of the business or job can obscure the needs of the client, and without guidance he or she goes back to the default behavior that caused trouble in the first place. Until my client's new ways of thinking and behaving become the norm, it's essential I make sure they implement the lessons and insights learned in our sessions together. I use a series of different methods and approaches, including something as simple as nudging them with emails. But perhaps the most effective way of keeping up with the client is through a set of forty-eight cards. Printed on each one is a question. For example, "Respect—Is it easy for me to give?"; "Imposter—Am I?"; "Past—Am I held hostage by it?" I urge my clients to keep a journal or blog (web log) of their responses so we can review them during our next session. Short of me riding around in their pockets every day, this is the best way to make sure my clients continue to think about our conversations and make progress on their own. The deck works on two other levels as well. It increases my client's self-awareness (the importance of which I explain in chapter 4) and it provides me with a rich source of information that allows me to understand more about the client's view of himself and the world.

STCT: THE PROCESS IN PRACTICE

There are four steps to completing the STCT process:

1. Contact
2. Assessment

3. Working Through
4. Closure

Contact

My initial meetings with clients most often takes place in their offices and last approximately two hours. During the course of the meeting I explain the nature of my work and take a history. This includes questions about their background (previous employment, former roles in the company); the problem at hand (to what degree does the problem impact the client's performance?); whether the difficulty is part of a pattern (has it happened before in similar circumstances?); and their business goals and objectives. I do my best to speak each client's language to make sure I understand what they are trying to achieve. During this meeting I also assess the clients' motivation to change and do the work required. Are they committed to developing the best in themselves? Are they self-motivated? And, most importantly, do they *really* want to change? As with any form of psychotherapy, I cannot change a client—they can only change themselves.

During this meeting, I also focus on my clients' communication style—what they say and how they say it—as well as what they don't say. For example, are there areas they avoid discussing? I observe their body language. Their emotional responses to my questions are also important. Finally, I take a good look at their offices. The way in which we shape our physical environment reflects and reinforces who we are.[12] Many individuals try to make offices their own by decorating them with pictures, photos, or keepsakes. These identity claims reinforce a person's sense of self and help in the process of personification by which a person maintains his or her sense of self within a team or business.[13] For example, Sara had a large poster of Rosa Parks in her office. For her, Parks represented courage and conviction, and seeing her on the wall every day helped Sara stand firm in her struggle to be taken seriously as a businesswoman. In addition to using decoration to reinforce our own sense of self we may choose to display objects that have a shared meaning, that make statements to others about how we would like to be perceived.[14] These statements may convey the truth to visitors about what we are really like, or deliberately offer up a more desirable persona. Our office can also reveal negative things about us. Michael, for example, was a hotshot manager of a Microsoft field office. There was no doubt in anyone's mind that he was going places, but he couldn't connect with his leadership team. People respected him yet found him cold and intimidating, and most thought he was only using his current position as a stepping-stone to something bigger. This perception was exacerbated by the décor in his office. The only personal item to be found was a printout of several customer tenets nailed into a wall. The books on his shelves were not his—they had been left by the previous manager—and there were no other clues to his identity. No family photos. No posters. Upon entering his office Michael's employees absorbed two messages. One, he was passionate about serving the customer, and two, he probably wasn't be going to be around very long before he moved on to a bigger job. They were right on both counts.

Toward the end of the contact stage I assess whether the client has the right stuff to be successful. This means:

- They acknowledge there is a problem to be solved and don't blame the job or someone else for their current situation. There are no victims in my practice. Each and every one of my clients must realize they have caused their own particular problem or difficulty. Our work will not be effective if a client feels he or she has been forced or coerced to see me, or if they view therapy as a requirement for promotion.

• They are self-motivated and prepared to work outside the confines of our one-on-ones together.

• They are prepared to open themselves to new ways of experiencing themselves and others. This often means letting go of thoughts, beliefs, and behaviors to which they may be attached.

• They see therapy as a process, not a quick fix. Leaders in Microsoft are chronically impatient to see how much they can achieve and how fast. As one Microsoft leader observed, "We plant seeds, then dig them up every couple of days to see if they are growing." This mindset doesn't gibe with the aims of STCT. I am all for making sure we emphasize the short nature of the therapeutic process but any clients coming to see me for a quick fix are usually disappointed. They need to commit to the process, leaving the seeds in the ground to grow and flourish. Learning to delay impulsivity is often an unexpected but welcome by-product of the therapeutic process.

Assessment

The assessment phase can take several forms. The first is usually a 360 evaluation, a leadership diagnostic completed by everyone, and I mean everyone, a client works with—their manager, direct reports, peers, colleagues, even customers. The 360 is a critical tool in assessing a client's awareness, confidence, and effectiveness. I based it on the work of Timothy Leary, who, before he urged a generation of hippies to "Turn on, tune in, drop out," was conducting breakthrough work as a psychologist at Harvard University.[15] Leary's methodology suits my practice because it operationalizes the interpersonal theory of psychology developed by Harry Sullivan. The result of the 360 pinpoints the characteristics of the leader's behavioral style and the likely effect that behavior will have on others. For example, Max's replies on his 360 may indicate that he perceives himself as having an interpersonal style that stresses leadership, energy, power, and expertise balanced with collaboration and support. He believes his behavior communicates the message, "I am a strong, competent, knowledgeable person on whom you can rely for effective guidance and leadership." From these self-perceptions I can extrapolate that Max is likely to be emotionally resilient, has a high level of self-belief, both in his own capability and that of his team, and realizes that the team approach is one of the most effective ways of getting things done. Based on Max's replies, it would also appear that his style inspires respect, obedience, and support from others. However, on the same 360, Max's colleagues and subordinates reveal that they perceive him as a hostile nonconformist. They feel he rarely includes them in any decision-making process and when they do get involved he discounts their contributions. The vast divide between how Max sees himself and how his directs see him tells me that he has a huge self-awareness problem—he is unaware of (or perhaps doesn't care about) the impact his behavior has on his team and others around him. This discrepancy provides Max and me with a good starting point for our work together because now I know that I need to break down the reasons for his lack of self-awareness. Does he lack awareness of the ways in which his behavior impacts others, or does is his self-absorption mask a more fundamental problem of low self-confidence? Clearly, his initial presenting problem—"People in my team are not performing as well as they should, they are always looking to me for guidance and insight"—is not the source of his woes, but merely a symptom of something bigger.

Sometimes a 360 isn't warranted. The client may have recently completed a different assessment and be unwilling to ask others for feedback again. She may be new to the company and people may not have had enough time to get a complete picture of her leadership style. Occasionally, a leader confesses an inability to handle hearing such raw truths from people they will have to look in the eye later that day. For these cases I have developed a series of exercises which, while not as comprehensive as a 360, also give me a good overview of the source of a client's problem. One exercise that works well, particularly with clients who are struggling with managing their relationships, is to ask them to write an essay about themselves using the third person. The narrative approach to psychotherapy has become an important adjunct in my own and many other therapists' work, and it is particularly important when communicating your beliefs, as we shall see in chapter 2.

Making my client think about himself in the third person enables me to assess how self-aware a client is. Can he see the world through other people's eyes? Who does he write about and what situations does he choose to discuss? Is he overly critical of his own performance or does he have a balanced view? An additional benefit to the third person perspective is that it has been shown to result in more positive, realistic appraisals of behavior.[16]

Brian was a client who had trouble asserting himself and using his power. Here is his essay with my interpretations included in parentheses.

"Imagine you were to shadow yourself for a day. What might you see? How did you behave? What feedback might you give yourself at the end of the day?"

One imaginary day two weeks ago I was Brian's shadow, poor me. (Humor or self-depreciation—lack of confidence?). I observed him during three distinct meeting types: some 1:1s, a team meeting, and a cross-organizational meeting.

The 1:1

Brian seems more at ease in his 1:1 interactions (What is different in his larger meetings—why is he less at ease?). He's relaxed and casual. Sometimes he jokes, sometimes he kvetches, sometimes he just listens. I was surprised to see how fluid the meeting was. (Positive insight. Build on this encouraging appraisal.) Some of his 1:1 meetings are highly structured, with a clear agenda, status briefs, and review of plans. Others are just conversations. Brian reinforced with at least one employee that the 1:1 was her time and she could fill it mostly as she liked. But I wonder if he shouldn't standardize the format more to make it easier for his employees to know what is expected of them. (Has the ability to empathize and take another's perspective.) Brian does tend to give his 1:1 partners his full attention during these meetings—shutting off his monitor, ignoring people at the door, for the most part ignoring calls—but I did see him take a call during one of his meetings. He apologized but I wonder if that made the employee feel somehow less of a priority. (Ruminative worry. Brain was aware of the problem and apologized. Needs to make a decision as to whether he takes calls or not.)

The Team Meeting

Brian's team meeting is in a small six-person conference room. Cozy. At the meeting I observed one of his leads brought cake and begged everyone to eat it all before the end of the meeting. This spawned a conversation about the kind of cake, who made it (the lead and her sons), who liked or didn't like chocolate cake, who liked or didn't like chocolate in other forms and various comments about striving to eat healthy while avoiding personal weaknesses. Brian didn't take an active role in the conversation because he was writing agenda items on the white board. (No agenda circulated prior to the meeting—wastes time and doesn't manage expectations.) While he didn't seem to mind the banter, he clearly wanted to get the meeting started and so did? (Either wants the meeting to start or wants the banter can't have both—needs to make a decision and stick to it.) Instead of just saying, "Let's get started," he asked how everyone was, which inspired yet more casual conversation about weekend activities, radiation therapy, and infant sleep. (Again, more focused on feelings than task—does Brian have a need to be liked/approved? Is this the reason for his passivity—he wants to be seen as a good guy, sympathetic and understanding? Also the use of an open-ended question, "How is everybody," conspires against the desire to start the meeting. Seems conflicted when it comes to asserting his own needs.) When I checked my watch to see how far into the hour we were it was eight minutes past. I wonder if Brian could make sure the time is used more efficiently? (No wondering about it—in an hour long meeting it's important to use the time efficiently and as Brain is the leader he owns the way the time is used. Need to get him to take more ownership/action.)

The X-Org Meeting

I also observed Brian during what turned out to be a contentious cross-organization meeting. I believe that one of Brian's team members was the meeting owner but I'm not quite sure because after 15 minutes or so into the meeting, Brian kind of took over. (Distances self from decision to take over.) I think his intention was to make sure his team was protected/supported but the result may have been that they felt a bit undermined. (Focus on feelings and impact. Needs to become more comfortable coming to the fore and making a decision—can always follow-up with team to explain behavior and also use as coaching for directs as to what they need to do so he doesn't have to step-in).

Now, I could just tell Brian that his third-person narrative reveals a sensitive man who is overly focused on the needs of others rather than on what he needs to do to get the job done. But why tell Brian when I can show him in black and white? Reading his annotated journal allows Brian to see first-hand what his own language reveals about the workings of his mind. The journal now also serves as a guide for what steps we need to take. For example, the journal starts off by describing Brian-the-observer as "poor me." I ask Brian why he feels compelled to use such self-deprecating humor. After giving the matter some thought, Brian realizes that rather than a simple off-the-cuff joke, his comment actually reveals that he just doesn't find himself particularly interesting. So the first step in helping Brian improve as a leader is to increase his confidence and make him more aware of his power and expertise. We do this by focusing on his strengths first. I point out that he seems very comfortable in his one–on-one meetings, adding value, managing the relationship, and being fully focused. I add that in these situations he is able both to manage the task at hand—providing value to his direct—and support the relationship. This is different to his larger meetings where he seems more focused on how people feel. We look in more detail at how he can run his larger meetings more like his more intimate one-on-ones. He identifies several areas he can work on. He feels more in control of the smaller meetings, more prepared and more relaxed. A key insight is that he sees the one-on-ones more as a conversation, whereas in the team meetings he is in a clear leadership role. Over the course of the next few weeks Brian works on identifying his expert power—the experience, skills, and talents he can bring to his team meetings, which he so effortlessly uses in his individual meetings—and manage the meeting more effectively by circulating an agenda beforehand.

THE DEVELOPMENT BLUEPRINT

After completing the 360 or another exercise, my client completes a Development Blueprint—a goal-oriented 30-, 60-, or 90-day plan that links therapeutic goals with business objectives. The Blueprint acts as a contract between me and my client and is another tool I use to keep in touch in between sessions. It helps clients identify the opportunities for development they have in their day-to-day activities and identify role models they can shadow and observe in action. This way, I know what my client is working on, when, and with whom. An example of a completed Blueprint is summarized in appendix 3.

Working through

Working through is a period during which the client engages in the heavy lifting of growth and development. We meet weekly for four or five sessions to assess progress against the Blueprint. During this time I will also shadow my client to assess how the problem behavior may manifest itself in specific situations. This allows me to give real-time feedback about the impact their behavior is having on others, and what they can do to change it. Each session is results oriented. It's during this period that we'll start assessing the client's levels of power or influence, or their preferred interpersonal style. I offer behavioral "prescriptions" and "homework." These keep the client working even when we're not together and act as a bridge between one session and the next.

Closure

During this final phase the client reflects on the process he has experienced in therapy. What progress has been made? What major insights have been revealed about his behavior? How confident does he feel that he can overcome setbacks in the future?

Traditional therapists use the word termination to describe the end of the therapeutic relationship. "Termination" sounds like an abrupt halt to the process. The message to the client is, "When you're done, you're done. It's over." I don't subscribe to this view, which is why I prefer the term closure. Closure implies the ending of one chapter and holds open the possibility of another. In my experience with STCT, I find that my clients are almost always ready to move on and become self-reliant. If a client wants to come back into therapy at some time in the future, I do not see that as a weakness or relapse. Should people who return to see their physician or dentist for more care be viewed as treatment failures?[17] Of course not. My approach is "once a client always a client," and I make sure the people I've worked with feel free to contact me at any time afterward, although, as a rule of thumb, I prefer them to wait three to six months to make sure they clarify and consolidate the gains they have made.

FIVE EASY PIECES

As we've discussed, Short Term Corporate Therapy provides a unique opportunity to engage in a rich exploration into the beliefs, behaviors, and thought processes that drive us in our professional lives. This book explores the five most universal obstacles to great leadership I have seen in my practice over the past twelve years. My intention in each chapter is threefold:

1. To give a birds-eye view of STCT in practice.
2. To demystify many of the psychological problems experienced by people in the workplace, and show that many successful people have overcome problems with beliefs, confidence, self-awareness, trust, and power.
3. To offer a process whereby the reader can use some of these techniques to become their own therapist or, perhaps, consider inviting a therapist into their corporation or business.

Through this book I guide you through some of the most common and some of the most disruptive emotional and behavior problems people experience at work. To get the most out of this relationship, heed the same advice I offer my clients: Commit to the process. Be open. Be honest. And be fearless in your desire to understand more about yourself. At the end of each chapter you'll find questions and exercises that will help you complete each stage of Short Term Corporate Therapy and discover more about your beliefs, your self-awareness, your confidence, your levels of trust, and your relationship with power.

As Mark Epstein, a Buddhist scholar and psychiatrist observes, many people go through life as if they are holding a coin with their fist tightly closed, rather than holding the coin in the palm of their hand.[18] I have met many leaders whose insecurities or anxieties cause them to clench their fists tightly around themselves, their team, or their business, stifling innovation and impairing effectiveness. Through STCT, these same people gain the confidence to hold their team in the palm of their hand, encouraging growth, risk, and trust. Allow the lessons and experiences provided by the men and women in this book to open your fist and release your true potential.

STCT: THINGS TO THINK ABOUT

STCT Refresh: STCT is designed to improve leaders' performance by improving their psychological health and well-being. It does this by focusing on three areas: (a) self-actualization—the ability of a person to fully exploit their talents, capabilities, and potential; (b) subjective well-being—the experience of happiness and exuberance; and (c) resilience—the ability to rebound from stress or adversity, to be steeled, not scarred, by experience.

The following six questions will help you learn more about yourself and how you might benefit from STCT.

1. Do you have a plan to enhance or improve your leadership effectiveness? Is it gathering dust in a drawer or do you consciously use it to manage your growth and development? Are you focusing on treating the symptoms that impact your performance, or are you tackling the core problem? What is the problem you are trying to solve? Be specific. Be sure to share the content of your plan with your manager and enlist her support.

2. If you don't have any kind of plan, look at the questions in appendix 3. These questions are the same ones Microsoft leaders answer during their 360 evaluations. Be honest. Share your responses with a couple of trusted advisors. Listen to their feedback. Do they agree with your self-assessment?

3. Shadow yourself for a day and write down your observations in the third person. What do you see? How do you behave? Is there anything you wish you could change about the way you act at work? What behaviors might you stop doing? Are there conversations you wish you could do over? Is there a pattern to the situations that trigger behavior you would like to change?

4. If you have direct reports, do they have development plans? Are you familiar with the content of these plans? Can you support them?

5. Unless you are independently employed, it's likely you work with a team. If your team were a family, how would you describe it? Close? Rambunctious? Competitive? Where do you fit in? For example, are you the dutiful oldest daughter, the attention-starved middle child, or the aloof father? Are you satisfied with your role? Who would you rather be? What could you do to change people's perception of how you contribute to the team?

6. To help you mirror as closely as possible the therapeutic experience my clients have when they see me initially, consider the following questions:

    a. How might you make life difficult for yourself at work?

    b. What is the feeling you most often experience when you are at work?

    c. What does it take for you to give up on a relationship, project, goal, or objective?

    d. Are you the person you thought you would become?

    e. Do you feel you are held hostage by events or experiences from your past that you can't forget or let go of?

2

Belief

The Cornerstone of Your Business

"We are defined by years of fun and boredom, of excitement and terror, of pleasure and pain, of love and loathing. Some portion of weathering and scars are visible. Some lie much deeper. . . . We are a product of the things we controlled as well as stuff that landed on our laps courtesy of fate, chance, bad luck or destiny."[1]

"You've got to believe in your product . . . you've got to believe in your work. Only a deep belief will generate the vitality and energy that give life to your work."[2]

DO YOU BELIEVE?

It promised to be a long, arduous day. The leadership team of one of Microsoft's online businesses was gathered to present the highly anticipated three-year plan that would outline how they intended to beat their major competitors. The room buzzed with energy as their audience settled into their chairs, an eager crowd of about sixty high-level managers who would be responsible for communicating the plan throughout the company. I sat in the back row. The leaders had asked me to attend their presentation, then meet with the managers separately to find out their honest reaction to what they had heard.

The leaders conducted their presentation with aplomb, projecting what to me was a mind-numbing array of charts and graphs to back up their numbers and predictions. The managers, however, seemed to appreciate this dense amount of data. They appeared interested, eager to hear more. They asked a lot of questions. Yet the more the leaders talked, the more I felt that initial buzz of energy the managers had carried in with them seep away.

Afterwards, the leaders left and I took their place, facing the managers from the front of the room. I had originally thought to begin by asking the group the obvious question, What did they think about the plan? But now I knew the real question that needed to be answered. So I asked, "Do you believe you're going to win?"

First there was confused silence. Then a few people piped up. "What do you mean by winning?" "Do you mean can we win or will we win?"

I rephrased the question. "Given everything you have heard today, do you believe you will beat the competition?" A small number of hands hesitantly went up. No more than six or seven people, 10 percent of the managers, believed this plan would work.

When the leadership team returned, I asked them the same question: How many of you believe this plan will allow you to beat your competitors? Only two hands went up!

This exercise, which allowed each group to know what the other one believed, launched a vigorous, passionate discussion. Now the managers felt empowered to voice their opinions. Now the executives were willing to consider ideas from the people who would be on the front lines. The plan that eventually launched was one every person in that room could put their heart and soul behind, one that was worth the hours of work and sweat it would take to achieve their goals. It was a plan they all believed in.

Since that meeting, the question of belief has become part and parcel of the division's business vocabulary. For people to get excited and invested in what they are doing, they have to believe in it. And they have to believe that their leaders believe in it. The belief has to be wholehearted, too, because believing in something halfway doesn't provide the motivation necessary to forge ahead when things get tough. Understanding what we believe—about ourselves, the world, our work—is the crucial first step to becoming a great leader.

WHY ARE BELIEFS IMPORTANT?

Without their beliefs, people would drift through life without an anchor. Our beliefs are at the very heart of what makes us unique, what makes me "me" and you "you." They are directly linked to our ability to fully exploit our potential and find personal and professional happiness. To be clear, the beliefs we'll discuss in this book have little to do with religious faith or spirituality. While religious belief often plays an important part in a person's approach to work, as we'll see later in this chapter, the beliefs that predominantly affect how we make sense of the world around us transcend the sacred.

Beliefs stem from our life experiences, particularly our turning points—those events that have forced us to make choices that not only changed the course of our future but revealed what we really care about. The beliefs molded by these turning points shape our perceptions of the world, influencing how we make decisions, what we focus on and what we ignore. They shape our attitudes, biases and assumptions, our values and what we value.[3] Rarely do people take the time to thoroughly examine or even identify the turning points in their lives, but when they do they're often stunned at how much these events drive their behavior. They discover why they feel comfortable making decisions in their professional lives yet waffle in their personal lives, or why they failed to see certain opportunities yet easily recognize others. Beliefs also impact the way we perceive ourselves, particularly our response to success and failure and the confidence we have in our ability to succeed.

BELIEFS IN BUSINESS

There are many ways in which our beliefs affect the way we approach our work, goals, relationships, and professional identity. In fact, there is a direct correlation between professional success and a strong set of beliefs. For example, Richard Branson, the charismatic chairman and founder of the Virgin group, observes in his autobiography, *Losing My Virginity*,[4] "It is my belief that every minute of every day should be lived as wholeheartedly as possible and that we should always look for the best in everyone and everything." In his relentless pursuit of this belief Branson is prepared to defy traditional business practice. Rather than follow the convention that shareholders are a company's first priority and customers and employees follow, Virgin does the opposite. "Employees matter most," Branson explains. "It just seems common sense to me that if you start off with a happy workforce, you're more likely to have happy customers. And in due course the resulting profits will make your shareholders happy." Branson's beliefs in a customer-centric, employee-friendly company can be seen at all levels, from the way he can be found serving customers dinner on one of his transatlantic flights to the fact that he starts every day reading and responding to e-mails from his employees. He has created a company where customers are willing to choose Virgin over competitors even when it would seem in their best interests to go with the other guys. For example, many people have said that when given the choice between a flight with a layover on Virgin, and a direct flight with another carrier, they will still choose Virgin. That's how good the service is.[5]

Microsoft is no stranger to the importance of having a set of clearly held beliefs. Employees in the company are passionate in their belief about changing the world. Early in my consulting career I was asked by the General Manager of the UK subsidiary what I thought were the reasons for Microsoft's success. He added that he had been asked to give a speech to the UK banking community about the company's "Secret Sauce" and was interested in my viewpoint. I thought then, and still believe now, that the reason for the company's accomplishments was the unshakable belief employees have in the company and in their ability to make a difference in people's lives. Belief is a fundamental part of the Microsoft culture and is embedded in the core DNA of company founders Steve Ballmer and Bill Gates. For Ballmer, running Microsoft requires much more than energy and commitment; it is a calling, an article of faith.[6] "You've got to be very realistic about where you are, but very optimistic about where you can be . . . and the day you can't be both of those things, you shouldn't be a leader of a company like Microsoft. You have to believe; you have to believe; you have to believe."[7]

You can also have a strong set of misguided or faulty beliefs. Jeffrey Skilling of the now-defunct Enron certainly had strong beliefs. He is reported to have said, "All that matters is money . . . you buy loyalty with money. This touchy feely stuff isn't as important as cash. That's what drives performance."[8] Skilling, it would seem, believed that greed is good. We all know where that belief got him and the company.

For years *Business Week* and *Forbes* were falling all over themselves to praise Skilling. For six years running Enron was voted "Most Innovative" among *Fortune's* "Most Admired Companies." In the same survey Enron also "topped the quality of management category"[9]; the *New York Times* called the company "a model for the new American workplace"; and *Business Week* named Kenneth Lay, Skilling's predecessor, one of the "top 25 managers of 2000." But any psychologist worth his salt could have told you Ken Lay was a train wreck waiting to happen. There are beliefs that drive self-actualization and positive mental health and those that create fear, uncertainty, and doubt. As you read through this chapter, consider whether your beliefs are a force of good—for you, your customers, and your business—or whether they are driven by narcissism, insecurity, ego, or greed.

GETTING OTHERS IN THE KNOW

It's not enough to know what we believe. Others have to know it, too. Good leadership is sometimes defined as the ability to get people to follow. I don't agree. Getting people to follow you is a byproduct of getting people to believe in you and in what you stand for. How you express what you believe—in words and actions—frames what your teammates, subordinates, or customers can expect from you, which in turn gives them the freedom to make significant decisions, not only regarding the ins and outs of their job, but whether to trust your leadership.

In the short term, articulating your beliefs to yourself and others will help you:

- Avoid just-in-time leadership. This is when you allow employees, colleagues, or partners to find out what you believe only at the last possible minute. Some managers use this tactic as a means of control; some to keep people on their toes. But in the end, all of the energy employees spend looking over their shoulders or preparing twelve versions of a project to anticipate your whims is energy they could funnel into doing their job better. In Microsoft this leadership behavior is called the *Seagull Call*—the leader "swoops down, craps all over you, and then flies away leaving his subordinates up to their knees in guano." A clearly articulated set of beliefs decreases the likelihood of surprises, allowing people to know what to expect from you and when, what matters to you and why, and how they can best contribute to the team's success.

- Prevent the drag on morale and goodwill that occurs when people are told they haven't lived up to expectations of which they weren't even aware.

- Provide the opportunity for employees to decide whether they want to work with you in the first place. It's up to you to attract people with the best potential fit for your team. If you secretly believe the philosophy that drives Six Sigma is the answer to getting the best out of your employees, hiring someone from the Live and Let Live School of Business probably isn't in either of your best interests. Save everyone time and frustration by making it clear up front what your beliefs and expectations are. Working with a leader who has a clearly articulated set of beliefs will bring the best out in my team.

Short-term benefits are all well and good. However, it's the long-term benefits of establishing your beliefs for yourself and those you work with that will make the biggest difference in your career. Acknowledging your strong set of beliefs, and sharing them with others, allows you to:

- Create a vision
- Establish your brand
- Lead through change

Creating a Vision

Establishing a clear sense of what a company aspires to achieve or become—the vision—correlates with long-term success and profitability.[10] Yet while a vision has to inspire both the head and heart, it also has to align with a leader's core beliefs. Otherwise, it can be analogous to having one foot on the accelerator and one on the brake—there is a lot of heat and noise but little forward momentum as each force cancels the other out.

I witnessed how aligned beliefs and vision can inspire tremendous change during an assignment in Hyderabad, India. Hyderabad is the fifth-largest city in India, a booming center of technological innovation and a city at the new frontier of commerce, industry, and software development. I'd been invited to Hyderabad to work with the senior leadership team in charge of improving one of Microsoft's remote development centers. They had just recruited their one thousandth employee and wanted to consolidate the leadership team and build the effectiveness of the organization. Most of the team were Microsoft veterans, some of whom had spent up to fifteen years with the company in the United States, who had returned to their country of origin for the reasons many of us go home: to raise children, to be near extended family and aging parents, to set down roots. But there was another reason I had yet to discover, a belief that would play an unprecedented role in my work with this particular group.

It was strange to walk around a Microsoft office designed and decorated in a very western fashion (the building itself would not look out of place on the Microsoft campus in the West) in the middle of a bustling Indian city. Despite the western trappings there was no doubt I was in India. Inside, nearly all the women were dressed in saris and many had the bindi mark on their forehead denoting that they were married; Hindus coexisted with Christians and Muslims; employees played cricket on the grass surrounding the building; and the café served only various Indian curries. As I was to realize, the dichotomy between the western architecture and Eastern dress, religions, and mores highlighted the organization's biggest problem and biggest opportunity.

Like many Microsoft teams I had worked with, these leaders passionately believed that their work at Microsoft could do great things for people around the world. Unlike most, however, they had a profound sense of duty to contribute specifically to India's success. I had never come across this before. No one had ever said to me, "I work here because I want to make America successful," or "I want to win this project for France." This powerful and unique belief was key to why they had returned home.

But something was also missing. A long process of interviews, discussions, and Leadership 360s revealed that no one could articulate the organization's vision. I got a different answer every time I asked.

A vision provides the roadmap for where an organization wants to go. It's more than a goal—it's a quest that appeals to the head and the heart of the whole organization. You might not complete it, but you'll be better off for having tried. The disparate groups in Hyderabad needed a unifying vision, something exciting that everyone could feel a part of that would offer a glimpse of the company's future. Currently people had no clear picture of where they or the organization would be in five years. Their high hopes of contributing great things to their country were being undermined by this lack of clarity. The leadership would need to establish a vision that would provide greater coherence for the organization, increase their effectiveness, and also align with their employees' sense of patriotism.

I wrote a report for the vice president of the organization summarizing my findings and suggesting a series of next steps, the most important being to bring the leadership team together, away from the company's offices, to craft the vision of the organization. This vision would have to fulfill several purposes:

- It had to outline an exciting Big Hairy Audacious Goal[11] that everyone could get behind for the long term.
- It had to address the problems and opportunities stemming from their unique circumstances and location—an emerging market in India.
- It had to establish their brand. Right now team leaders were expected to take any programming job that filtered down from Microsoft headquarters in Redmond, Washington. This beggars-can't-be-choosers approach was breeding some resentment, as their perception was that they only got what the developers in Redmond didn't want to handle. They needed to show Redmond what they were best at, and insist on accepting only the projects that furthered their agenda and worked for the good of the company.
- It had to be built on the unshakable belief that in addition to providing value to Microsoft and its shareholders, the center's purpose was to provide wealth and success for India.

After a two-day offsite the team had composed the first draft of a vision that fulfilled the above criteria. It also demanded a company-wide reorganization that would transform the center from a disparate set of businesses to a hub of engineering excellence over the next five years. They also gained the confidence to push back and become more self-directed. That is, they learned to say no to Redmond.

Since then, other remote development centers in China and Israel have begun to follow India's lead. They have learned that identifying a team's core set of beliefs and running their business accordingly, rather than trying to be a jack-of-all-trades, is the surest path to better market share, profit, and growth.

Establishing Your Brand

As the team in Hyderabad learned, our beliefs are also our branding tool. That's how they were able to establish themselves as Microsoft's go-to division instead of their division of last resort. Identifying what makes us unique is not about marketing what we've done; it's about announcing who you are. In a world that is becoming more homogeneous, your beliefs *are* your unique brand, built on your life experiences. No one else has been through what you have, seen what you have seen, or done what you have done. I find it ironic when my clients come to me hoping to craft a unique personal brand simply by differentiating themselves from the brands of their coworkers ("Evelyn is the calm in the storm; Jeff is the go-to guy; I should be the renegade."). It will never work. To create a meaningful and unique brand, we have to tap the rich seam of the life experience that formed our beliefs.

Creating a unique personal brand has a number of significant benefits. Because the process involves a considerable degree of soul searching it increases self-awareness. It also "lets you control how other people perceive you," writes Peter Montoya, author of *The Brand Called You*.[12] By communicating your brand, he explains, "You're telling them what you stand for, but in a way that's so organic and unobtrusive that they think they've developed that perception all by themselves." Your brand also helps build trust. People understand what matters to you, what gets you out of bed in the morning, so they are less likely to be blindsided by your behavior or your expectations. After all, the best predictor of how someone will behave in the future is to observe how they have behaved in the past.

A clearly established, passionately pursued personal brand can be the genesis for leadership success on a much broader scale. Most successful companies, whether large or small, owe a tremendous debt to founders who insisted on weaving their beliefs into the fabric of the organization. Two companies I've always admired are Patagonia, which produces garments and tools for outdoor sports, and Doyle Dane Bernbach (DDB), the revolutionary ad agency founded in the late 1940s.

Patagonia was founded on the beliefs of Yvon Chouinard, mountain climber, surfer and social activist. Originally a self-taught blacksmith, Chouinard transformed the process of mountain climbing by forging hard-steel pitons he then sold from the back of his car (a piton is a steel spike that is hammered into cracks to create an anchor to which climbers can attach their ropes). To Chouinard's dismay, however, within a few years the success of the pitons was having a detrimental impact on the mountains he loved. Too many people were using them and leaving them behind, littering the rock face and damaging the rock itself. His decision? To stop manufacturing the very item that contributed 70 percent toward his bottom line. He then committed his company to developing a new, removable piton that climbers could reuse. Chouinard built an organization whose brand is an extension of his life experiences, experiences that forged his strong beliefs in environmental activism, personal responsibility, and self-actualization. He explains:

> I realize now that I was trying to instill in my company the lessons I'd already learned as an individual and as a climber, surfer, kayaker, and fly-fisherman. . . . Never exceed your limits. You push the envelope, and you live for those moments when you're right on the edge, but you don't go over. You have to be true to yourself; you have to know your strengths and limitations and live within your means. The same is true for a business. The sooner a company tries to be what it is not—the sooner it tries to "have it all"—the sooner it will die.[13]

True to his word, Chouinard has created a company that is true to his beliefs. When Patagonia grew to the point at which it was forced to rely on ecologically suspect manufacturers in order to meet client demand, Chouinard scaled back rather than abandon his commitment to the environment. He reduced his product line and helped farmers eager to work with Patagonia become pesticide-free. He also laid off 20 percent of his employees.

Bill Bernbach was no less iconoclastic; both in his influence on the advertising world and on the advertising company Doyle Dane Bernbach, which he co-founded in the late 1940s. He believed in the essential goodness of people, courtesy, intuition, humility, and living life to the fullest. He "truly believed that advertising people more than any other ought to use their talents not just to sell, but to make the world a better place."[14] True to his beliefs, DDB was the first to hire ethnic minorities and women into visible and decision-making positions. He only insisted that the people hired fulfill two require-ments: They had to be talented and they had to be nice. "If you were nice but without talent, we were very sorry but you just wouldn't do," he observed.[15] "We had to 'make it,' and only great talent would help us do that. If you were a great talent but not a nice person, we had no hesitation in saying 'no.' Life is too short to sacrifice so much of it to living with a bastard." Bernbach passed away in 1982, yet the com-pany he co-founded still holds to his beliefs of courtesy, intuition, fierce creativity, and innovation. The current leadership recognizes that they "are a product of his [Bernbach's] imagination,"[16] and the agency remains true to Bernbach's belief that to be successful DDB has to be, by instinct and inclination, the enemy of the ordinary.

Joe is a good example of a Microsoft leader who has learned to use his beliefs to lead his business. Joe and I worked together to help him become a more visible leader in the company. An exceptionally good second-in-command, he wanted to be recognized for his own leader-ship impact and agenda. To accomplish this personal transformation he needed to refresh his brand so we spent some time looking back in order to move forward.

Joe completed a beliefs audit and it revealed a man who had expe-rienced some significant turning points in his life but had been steeled, rather than scarred, by them. The turning points he used to build his brand were: being sent away to boarding school as a small boy; his first job as a construction worker; and the death of his daughter when he was a manager in Microsoft.

His early experiences were of being unable to cope. He was bullied at boarding school for being different: he spoke English while his peers spoke Afrikaans; he came from town, they came from the tougher farming community. He decided that rather than accept his situation he "was going to change the way things were in [his] life." He became a star rugby player for the school and "after careful plotting invented a way to break out of the school at night." The school, he told me, was more like a juvenile prison, so escaping earned him the respect of everyone from that day forward.

Following school he enrolled in university. His parents couldn't afford his tuition so he took a part-time job as a construction worker at a large petrochemical factory in South Africa. The job, it turned out, was to be his stepping-stone into computers and on to Microsoft. He was discovered as the "computer expert" by management and went from hardhat to tie, from manual labor to "tapping on a keyboard."

His third turning point was the death of his daughter. He and his family had moved from South Africa to Microsoft corporate head-quarters in Redmond and soon after his daughter fell ill. Eighteen months later his daughter passed away and Joe blamed himself. "I wasn't a good enough parent—had I been better I would have been able to save her." His confidence as a manager plummeted and his weight ballooned to over 300 pounds. The community where he and his wife lived reached out to them and Joe's manager became a significant source of strength and support.

Looking back at these experiences Joe learned that on many occasions he believed or had been told he was not good enough or that a system or policy did not allow what he was trying to do, or it was not possible. But "it's not true . . . nothing is impossible." His beliefs are:

- Learning and enlightenment—the harder you think the more you will discover. It's never too late to find out how things work, or why they work the way they do.
- Think out of the box—nothing is impossible.

- Hard work pays off.
- Keep it simple and you won't forget it.
- My gut feel is very accurate.
- I am in charge of my own destiny.

From these he developed his brand that he uses to guide himself and his business:

- Thought leadership—drive ideas forward and lead, but always be prepared to listen to others.
- Innovation—don't accept the status quo. Be creative and think hard about new ways of being efficient and effective.
- Simplicity—complexity increases the risk of failure.
- Practicality—common sense must prevail.
- Get it done. Talking is all well and good but completion and execution matter most.

Leading through Change

The third long-term benefit of knowing our beliefs and living according to them is that they act as a beacon when we're sailing the rough waters caused by change. Big changes can also be referred to as life events. They include major shifts that impact our future, such as buying or selling a home, getting married, and starting or losing a job. Any life event, whether positive or negative, challenges our psychological status quo. The stress we experience is caused by the effort we use to cope and regain normal levels of health and well-being. There is a clear link between the numbers of life events a person experiences and their risk of suffering physical or emotional ill health.[17]

When I started working at Microsoft I was immediately struck by the scale and pace of reorganization and change. The company's normal state of affairs seemed to be one of almost perpetual transformation. The need to adapt to this seemingly endless cycle was so great that the leaders I spoke to labeled "dealing with ambiguity" as a key competence they had to excel at to be effective. This differed significantly from the stability of other companies I had worked with whose managers seemed to experience little in the way of change. I decided to see if my initial impressions, that these managers were dealing with a greater than ordinary amount of turbulence in their lives, were correct. I surveyed managers at Microsoft, and at the other companies I was working with, to determine the incidence of what I termed corporate life events—changes in team structure, for example, or changing managers; joining a new team; teams merging and breaking up; strategic or organizational changes. My results established that a Microsoft manager was eight times more likely to experience a corporate life event than his counterpart from the financial services sector—12.5 events compared to 1.5. The data suggested that Microsoft as a company was "life-event prone," a term coined by Ian Goodyear when studying families in which children were exposed to a greater number of major life changes than average due to parental illness.[18]

Knowing Microsoft was life-event prone helped shape my approach toward team therapy at the company. In an environment prone to frequent change, it seemed important to figure out what a leader could do to make sure that it didn't sap his and his team's will and morale. Exposure to stressful situations may do one of two things; it may sensitize or "scar" individuals, throwing them easily off-kilter when faced with highly stressful situations, or it may steel them in such a way that they become immune to the effect of stress or adversity.[19] Whether a person is scarred or steeled by serial change, adversity, or ambiguity depends on many factors. These include personality, whether one is optimistic or pessimistic; the strength of personal relationships within a team or business; and the ability of the leader to strengthen and reinforce his coping efforts. One significant way in which a leader can steel his team against the stress or disruption caused by serial change is by reinforcing his beliefs. The failure of many corporate change programs—large or small—can be traced directly to employee resistance.[20] One way to break down or avoid this resistance is for a leader to communicate his beliefs—openly and often. By framing any change in the context of his beliefs a leader provides an anchor for his employees to hold onto. In an ever-changing world, beliefs are a constant, honoring the past, connecting with the present, and providing hope for the future.

IDENTIFYING YOUR BELIEFS

So how do you begin to identify your beliefs and articulate them so others know what to expect of you? You need to go back in time so you can create a story that serves your future. It's a three-part process:

Step 1: Take inventory. Identify the turning points in your life, those events that forced you to make a choice and revealed what you strongly care about.

Step 2: Create a narrative. Identify a story that illustrates and explains your beliefs.

Step 3: Tell your story. For your team members, hearing, and seeing is believing.

Step 1: Take inventory

The key to understanding your beliefs is to identify the turning points that caused you to think or behave differently than you did before. Psychologists define a turning point as any event that shapes the course of your future, whether you know it or not. For example, Rosa Parks was faced with a turning point when she decided not to give up her seat to a white man. When Steve Jobs was fired from Apple, he could have sunk into a deep depression. Instead he says, "It freed me to enter one of the most creative periods in my life."[21] Similarly Howard Schultz, the coffee impresario, had no idea he was on his way to creating an empire when he decided to leave his lucrative New York job to join Starbucks, which at the time was a small start-up in the Pacific Northwest with only five stores.[22]

To help my clients take inventory of their turning points, I ask them a series of questions such as, "What have been some of your most significant life experiences? Why were they significant? What decisions did they force you to make? What did you learn about yourself? How do these experiences affect what kind of leader you are today? What do you value and what do you believe in?"

Monica was interested in identifying her brand. Naturally, this meant we had to first establish her beliefs. Our first step was to list the turning points of her life. These included refusing financial assistance from her parents in college; being dumped by the man for whom she had moved to Seattle; and finally, a job interview with the head of a very successful software company. This particular turning point played a big role in her subsequent belief system. She explained:

> It was more a religious experience than an interview. He didn't ask me
> any of the standard interview questions—we simply had a conversation

about beliefs and values. At the end of our conversation he told me of the Greek myth of Sisyphus. Sisyphus was doomed [for eternity] to push a rock up a hill [yet as soon as he almost reached the top, the rock would roll back down the hill]. While the actual story of Sisyphus is fairly depressing, this fellow took the myth and modified it in a way I found compelling and even life-changing. He explained that he viewed his entire career as the task of rolling the rock up the hill. Reaching the top of the hill [would mean he'd achieved] his life's ambition. "Where Sisyphus got it wrong," he explained, "was that he tried to roll the rock up the hill on his own. In order to get that rock up the hill I need help. I can't do it myself. And over the course of my career I find key people with unique talents to help me succeed in rolling the rock up the hill to accomplish something great in all of our lifetimes." I really took that belief, that sense of investment in others, to heart.

Monica told me, "I approach every business relationship as a long-term investment. . . . People are often too self-focused, and view relationships only at a single point in the time continuum. The collective group of folks helping one another is the only way to really make an impact, and to me, understanding this is a core principle of leadership."

Identifying the turning points in her life gave Monica insight into her beliefs, the building blocks with which she could create her brand, Intellectual Integrity. Next, she would craft a story so that she could share her beliefs with everyone.

Step 2: Create Your Narrative

The best tool for sharing your beliefs is narrative. A leader who knows how to tell a good story, one that entertains and inspires, can infuse a team, and even an entire company, with energy and a can-do spirit it might not otherwise have.

The power of narrative lies in its ability to excite us, to show us a better place, to educate, warn, or inform us. Bruno Bettelheim, the child psychiatrist who wrote about the power of fairy tales in his book the *Uses of Enchantment*,[23] commented that for a story to hold a child's attention it must not only entertain and arouse curiosity, but it must also stimulate the imagination. It must be attuned to anxieties and aspirations and suggest solutions to problems that concern her.

Adults require the same from their stories. And yet most business leaders I have worked with use PowerPoint, not narrative, to communicate their ideas and objectives. I'm sure this is the same in many companies around the world. Most leaders rely on the objective truths of analysis, facts, and figures. It quantifies their results. I think that many managers feel that transferring their ideas to a slide presentation immediately confers some authenticity or rigor to the content of their discourse. Using PowerPoint also allows some people to hide behind the slides, literally standing at arm's length away from the content. Now, there is nothing wrong with a finely crafted PowerPoint deck. They're great for communicating the facts and figures of a business, for example budget forecasts or profit summaries. But even the best deck cannot convey what a leader really stands for. As Stephen Denning, the former program director of Knowledge Management at the World Bank, comments, "Analysis might excite the mind, but it hardly offers a route to the heart and that's where we must go if we want to motivate people."[24]

I was reminded of Denning's advice when I visited my children's new school. It was a new parents evening. As I moved from classroom to classroom, each teacher dutifully fired up PowerPoint and spoke about the syllabus my children would be following. As the evening wore on I became more and more frustrated. I had little interest in the content of the syllabus. I had that already. What I wanted to know was some information about the teacher. His background and teaching philosophy, what I could expect from him, and what he needed from me. Toward the end of the evening, bored and looking forward to going home, I settled into the English teacher's class. The teacher introduced himself and started by telling us about his favorite books. I was interested. He then spoke about his background—where he went to school and what kind of a student he had been. I was hooked. I remember very little about my night prior to this presentation. But I remember everything about my daughter's English teacher—how literature had opened doors for him, why he wanted to teach, and most of all, his belief in the power of the printed word to stimulate young growing minds.

In his analysis of several of the world's top leaders Harvard cognitive psychologist Howard Gardner concluded, "The ultimate impact of the leader depends most significantly on the particular story he or she relates or embodies and the receptions to that story on the part of audiences."[25] Storytelling taps us at an emotional level. We believe what we hear in the form of a story. A University of California, Berkeley study asked MBA candidates to judge whether or not a company had a practice and policy of avoiding layoffs. Group One was told a story about how the company had responded during the last recession. Group Two was given statistical data showing that the company had significantly less involuntary turnover than their competitors did. Group Three was read a policy statement by the top executive. The study found that the MBA candidates, people who were being trained to trust numbers and solid data, believed the story over the statistics or policy statement. Data is important as a decision-making tool, but when it is time to convince people to follow, tell a story.

There are four steps to crafting a compelling story.

1. First, identify your story's purpose, what you want it to achieve, as this will determine its content. For example, we tell some stories to spark action and motivate people, others to share our knowledge and experiences about success and failure, and others to communicate who we are. Above all the story has to be believable—tall tales make the storyteller look good, but don't promote trust or motivation.[26]

2. Next, distill the narrative to make it short and succinct. There is nothing worse than a rambling, disjointed, boring story. A story doesn't have to be overly long but it does have to have a structure—a beginning, middle, and end. This can be accomplished successfully in a five- or ten-minute period. As an example, consider this very short story that Jack Welch, the ex-CEO of GE, tells in his memoir, *Jack: Straight from the Gut*.[27] He received a tongue-lashing from his mother after he hurled his hockey stick across the ice in response to a disappointing loss. "You punk!" she said. "If you don't know how to lose, you'll never know how to win." His story is spare on details but rich in emotion, authenticity, and lessons. We learn a lot about Jack Welch from this brief story—his passion for winning but his realization that failure is always a reality in life; that he took part in ice hockey as a kid; that his mother played a big role in his life. Small, or in this case short, is beautiful.

3. Paint a picture. Your audience has to be drawn in to the story. They have to be able to visualize the context, understand the characters, and experience the trials and tribulations of the storyteller. To keep the audience emotionally invested, leaders should own their story by using

personal pronouns such as "I" or "me." Don't distance yourself from the content by talking about "we" or "us."

4. End with a take-home message. An unsatisfactory conclusion can ruin the best story. It's anticlimactic and leaves people wondering why they listened in the first place.

For an example of how to put these four steps together, consider Barb's story. Barb reviewed the results of her leadership 360 and saw she had received low marks for storytelling. She hadn't been in the company long and was in the process of building her leadership team. She recognized that a story would help develop her relationship with members of her team, communicate her beliefs, and prepare the team for a major change initiative they were to lead worldwide. She identified a significant life experience that had caused her to think differently about the priorities in her life and set about crafting her story.

On the day she was to tell the story to her team she was nervous but determined. She began by setting the story's context and purpose. "Big hard physical goals appeal to me. I jumped out of an airplane and I've run a marathon—once was enough on both counts. I'm drawn to these high-risk activities because they demand a lot from me in terms of focus, training, and staying in the moment and enjoying the challenge, qualities that I believe are the key to achieving success in life. It was during the hardest physical challenge of my life, though, that I almost abandoned the principles that have always meant so much to me."

Barb then began to paint a vivid picture. "It was a bike ride from Montreal to Portland, Maine. I flew to Montreal the night before the event. I wanted to talk to some of the other riders, get to know them, but instead I went straight to my hotel room to get as much sleep as I could before the first day. I was worried that I couldn't handle the three days of 100+ miles in a row. The next day, everyone was smiling and wishing each other luck. Not me. I hunkered down and I focused. And I rode. I didn't talk very much, I didn't stop too often, and I didn't laugh. I rode right by the famous old covered bridges instead of stopping to go for a swim or take a photo."

She then reached the climax of her story. "On the last day, the easy 50-mile, flat, beautiful day, I hit the curb and took a spill. Down I went, bleeding profusely from my nose, elbow, and knee and nursing a hurt hand. I verified quickly that my nose probably wasn't broken, got back on my bike, and limped along to the next rest stop some five miles away."

Barb eventually finished the ride and, as she explained to her leadership team, learned some important lessons from the experience:

- The goal was a good one, and focusing on it was helpful. However, I forgot to enjoy myself.
- I had trained enough. I should have trusted that I would finish the ride. Yes, my legs hurt, my butt hurt, and I was tired, but what's the point if you're not having fun?
- I missed out by not talking to the other riders. Maybe they could have warned me about that tricky curve in the last fifty miles. Maybe I would have learned a new riding tip. Sharing the experience, the challenges, and the successes with others should always be part of the objective in any challenge.

And then came her punch line. "So why I am I telling you this story today? Because we are embarked on the transformation [of our business] and we have a great goal. We have completed our training by determining our vision and strategy for the organization and by getting the leadership community involved in the process. And now as we continue to go forth to the wider Microsoft community, I want to make sure that while we keep our eyes on the end goal, we don't miss the experience along the way. So talk to each other, talk to your wider community. Share what's working and what isn't. And stop to celebrate our successes and to look at the covered bridges."

I didn't time Barb's story but it only took between five and eight minutes. During this time her team learned a lot about who Barb was:

- She likes big challenges and isn't afraid to sign up for them.
- She is persistent and determined.
- She has a sense of humor.
- She recognizes that any endeavor worth doing is worth doing well and investing time in.
- She likes working with people.
- She wants people on her team to focus and work hard but to enjoy the journey on the way.

They also learned something about how Barb wanted them to lead the change initiative—together, sharing experiences and celebrating successes, but most of all remembering to look at the covered bridges. "Look at the covered bridges" became a rallying cry for the team.

Step 3: Tell Your Story

During the young athletes study I met an Olympic gymnast whose story would stay with me over the years. Mike had been training to be a gymnast since the age of five. As he grew older and began showing great promise as a professional athlete, winning awards and eventually joining the national team, his life became dominated by the sport. It was not uncommon for him to train fifty to sixty hours a week. Upon being invited to take part in the Young Athlete Study, Mike completed a battery of physical and psychological tests. I then visited him at home to learn more about his experiences as an elite young athlete. During one interview, I was surprised to learn that this talented athlete at the height of his career had a secret: Mike confided that he wanted to retire from the sport so he could have a "normal" life. The problem was that Mike's gymnastics meant everything to his father. His son's accomplishments defined him, gave him status in the community, and gave him a purpose. Mike was afraid to confront his father about his desire to quit the sport. Instead, his solution had been to leave travel magazines in plain view around the house, thinking that his father would see them and ask Mike why he was planning to travel. Unfortunately, Mike's dad ignored the clues, and Mike was still training. When the data collection portion of the research finished Mike was still training and competing. I often wonder how the story resolved itself and what Mike is doing now.

Leaders can't just leave their "magazines"—their clues—out there and hope people notice them. If you want to tell your story, to have people to listen to you, to believe in you, it's not enough to drop hints. You have to be direct. You have to be explicit. Otherwise, you have no one to blame for your ineffectiveness but yourself. To demonstrate the power of your beliefs you have to be prepared to be visible and operate above the radar so that people learn what you care about not just by what you do, but what you say.

One leader who truly understands his beliefs and knows how to tell a good story is Steve Jobs, the CEO of Microsoft's competitor, Apple. At a recent Stanford University commencement, Jobs framed his "Stay Young; Stay Foolish"[28] address through three stories from his life experience. One was about "connecting the dots" and focused on his early years—his adoption, dropping out of college, and the influence of calligraphy (an interest that was to shape the typography of the original Macintosh computer). The second story was about love and loss and recounted his rise and fall and then his rise again at Apple Computers when he went from founder, to being fired, to being recruited back into the company he had founded. The final story was about death and focused on the day he was diagnosed with incurable pancreatic cancer, a diagnosis that turned out to be incorrect—he had a very rare form of the disease, which was operable—but a diagnosis he lived with for 24 hours. He completed his address with these words:

> Your time is limited so don't waste it living someone else's life. Don't be trapped by dogma—which is living with the results of other people's thinking. Don't let the noise of others' opinions drown out your own inner voice. And most important, have the courage to follow your heart and intuition. They somehow already know what you truly want to become. Everything else is secondary.

Steve Jobs is a master at knowing how to use narrative and storytelling to communicate the beliefs he has acquired through his life experience. In this instance his message was rich in content; succinct (the whole speech took just over fourteen minutes); it was delivered with credibility and humility, and the content was *specific* to his audience. His fundamental belief in trusting oneself and having the courage to follow one's dreams despite what others might say certainly resonated with not only the audience who attended this address but many at Microsoft. It was a senior vice president in the company who first sent me the text of Jobs' speech.

Microsoft, too, is steeped in a rich storytelling tradition. Steve Ballmer believes that Microsoft is much bigger than a software company—it is a change-the-world company. He communicates this belief with such conviction that it's almost impossible for anyone else not to adopt it, and he has used this belief to inspire his employees, and even bring them back from the brink of destruction. At the 2000 Microsoft annual briefing he used narrative to get a crowd of over 30,000 demoralized employees to chant *"Ali Bomaye, Ali Bomaye,"* the same chant that helped carry Muhammad Ali to one of his most famous victories, winning the World Heavyweight Championship against George Foreman. I never saw Ballmer's legendary perform- ance but I've heard about it from so many of the leaders I work with that I might as well have been there.

At the time, Microsoft was on the ropes. The Department of Justice was investigating whether the company had abused its monop- oly power, and many employees feared the company would be broken up. Anxiety at the company was high. There were reports of Microsoft employees being verbally and physically assaulted by people intent on taking "justice" into their own hands. Whereas once "Microsofties" would proudly wear the company logo on their clothes or computer bag, these external trappings of allegiance had become much rarer sightings both within and outside the company. To make matters worse, competitors were threatening to undermine the monopoly the government was investigating. These threats from all sides were taking their toll on the morale and competitive spirit of the company.

Showing clips of the landmark fight in which Ali conquered his greatest nemesis, Ballmer used story to share his belief in what Microsoft was capable of: courage, inspiration, commitment, daring; it was a story that no one could resist. His enthusiastic rhetoric—it's not that we might win or we can win, we *will* win!—touched the heart and soul of every person in that dank auditorium. Confronted with such a ferocious belief in the destiny of the company, Microsoft employees couldn't help but leave the meeting charged with a sense of invincibility. From then on, *"Ali Bomaye"* became the equivalent of a secret handshake. It's clear that after this meeting you would have been hard-pressed to find a single employee who wasn't giving 110 percent to their job, and smiling about it.

Ultimately, the decision to break up the company was overturned. Did Ballmer's belief in the company affect the outcome? Of course not. Would the company have survived such a rough patch and evolved into the juggernaut it is today without such fierce belief from its leaders? Impossible. A company is nothing without leaders who know how to inspire others to reach for extreme heights.

STAYING ABOVE THE RADAR

Interestingly, a lot of outspoken, idea-driven people who owe their professional success to being comfortable with telling stories and expressing their beliefs clam up once they start ascending to certain levels of success. Suddenly they can't get people to cooperate, and they're disappointed when their teams misunderstand their agenda or simply can't deliver what is asked of them. The flow of communication slows to a dribble and eventually stops.

The problem is that these managers are now flying under the radar. They become almost invisible to their colleagues and team members. Yet how can this be when the manager is more visible than they've ever been, with their corner offices and seats at the head of the conference table?

Often, when people reach high levels of power, they suddenly realize that everyone is listening to what they say, that their words and directives matter so much that they can affect the entire company and the liveli-hood of employees. That's a heavy responsibility, and it's easy for man-agers in these positions to become self-conscious and move to protect themselves from the burden of having to be right. They keep their true beliefs about the requisites for success to themselves so that no one can accuse them of misguiding the team should things go wrong.

The problem, of course, is that the vaguer you are about what you believe, the more people become anxious and uncomfortable and lose their trust in you. They're left trying to read the behavioral tea leaves to identify what success looks like and what they need to do to achieve it. No wonder they can't get things right! If your beliefs are rock solid, and you can articulate them in an inspiring and convincing way, you'll energize your team in such a way that even if problems do arise, they'll be prepared to handle them appropriately.

WHEN GOOD BELIEFS GO BAD

Like most things in life our beliefs evolve, mature, and sometimes decay. Sometimes they are replaced by insights provided by new expe-riences and learning. Some of these changes might represent a para-digm shift that necessitates seeing the world in a whole new way. For example, the Copernican revolution changed forever people's belief that Earth was the center of the universe. More recently, Nelson Mandela moved South Africa away from apartheid to conform to our ideas of what an integrated society looks like.

You want your beliefs to change. It's proof that you are keeping your eyes open, living fully, and welcoming everything that the world and people around you can teach you. Your good beliefs will likely go bad if you allow them to remain unchallenged.

We often neglect to perform reality checks on our beliefs until we're forced to do so by tragedy or misfortune. Take as an example the Columbia space shuttle explosion on February 1, 2003. NASA treated it as a horrible accident that couldn't have been prevented. Yet though NASA pled innocence, it wasn't the first tragedy to strike. On January 28, 1986, America was shocked by the explosion of the space shuttle Challenger, which killed its seven crewmembers. Following the Challenger accident President Reagan created a commission to look into the causes of the tragedy. The Rogers Commission concluded that while the physical cause of the accident was the failure of a small gasket no more than two inches in diameter, the NASA management was also at fault.[29]

The investigators pointed out that the success of putting a man on the moon had caused the space agency to rest solidly on its belief that it was "the best organization that human beings could create to accomplish selected goals."[30] The commission concluded that management and employees were "unable to recognize that NASA never had been, and still was not a perfect place." The Commission published its report in 1986, including a series of recommendations to ensure a tragedy of this nature would never happen again. Unfortunately, while many of the organizational recommendations were implemented, the misguided beliefs had become embedded in the culture of the agency and caused a gradual erosion of the safety systems and quality control that were to blame for the shuttle disaster. As one observer noted, "Beliefs held in common throughout the [NASA] organization were resilient and bounced back into shape after being stretched or bent."[31] Belief in NASA as the "perfect place" persisted as safety and quality eroded. By the time of the Columbia disaster, an organizational consultant described the leadership of NASA as exhibiting "flawed decision making, self-deception, introversion and a diminished curiosity about the world outside the perfect place." The deception persisted even in the face of conflicting evidence. On many occasions the engineers informed management that the foam tiles that protected the shuttle from extreme temperatures during reentry were unsafe and could cause "a catastrophic failure in the shuttle's heat shield." But the investigation into the Columbia accident found that the engineers' concerns about "risk and safety were competing with—and were defeated by—management's belief that foam tiles could not hurt the shuttle."

Both the Challenger and Columbia accidents highlight the danger of unchallenged, inflexible beliefs. In the case of the shuttle disasters there are many reasons why, even in the face of insurmountable evidence, the leadership continued to believe that the organization was perfect. No one, it seemed, wanted to admit that something couldn't or shouldn't be done, that resources were being stretched too thin. No one had the guts to stand up and say, "We can't make that date."[32] From the available evidence, NASA leadership circled the psychological wagons and persisted in a state of denial. In many ways the leadership of NASA preceded Enron as an example of how a set of unrealistic beliefs supported an organization that was doomed to fail.

Beliefs can be hard to change. It takes courage and no small amount of self-reflection to admit what drives our behavior. It takes even more guts to replace old, faulty beliefs with new ways of thinking and behaving. You have to check in every now and then to make sure that the beliefs you hold are still relevant, or that you haven't compromised what you believe in. If you remain blind to how your beliefs shape and drive your behavior you are doomed to make the same mistakes over and over again. No matter how compelling your narrative is, if your behavior is at odds with what you say you will lose credibility and good will. It is important to conduct a regular health check, a Reality Test, of your beliefs to make sure they aren't putting you, your business, or your organization at risk. We will review how to conduct a Reality Test in chapter 3.

CHANGING WHAT WE BELIEVE

Our beliefs can also change due to circumstance or experience. Rajiv, a senior leader, was passionate about self-improvement and thought working with me would help him become a more effective manager. The results of his 360 revealed a man who cared deeply for his people and who had built a strong leadership team, but the verbatim feedback from his direct reports was that they needed him to be clearer about what he stood for. In order to achieve this objective we had to begin by identifying the beliefs that underpinned his convictions.

Rajiv completed a Beliefs audit that brought to light some significant turning points in his life. As a boy he had been saved from drowning in the most holy river in India, the Ganges; as a young man he had failed to get into his, and his parents', dream college; and more recently, he had been forced to leave a job that he loved and where he excelled because of a poor relationship with his manager, who had gone so far as to ask him to lie to cover up some weaknesses in the business. This last turning point, he realized, had changed everything for him.

When he had begun his career at age 22, he believed that money was the ultimate reward for work. Money was his first priority, followed by job satisfaction, family, and self-realization. Now, twelve years later, as he thought about what he had learned from his bad work experience, he realized that his beliefs had changed and as a result so had his priorities. The bad experience with his manager showed him that money and power could not provide lasting happiness, and that success could take many forms, not all of them visible to outsiders. These insights caused him to change his belief from "Money is the ultimate reward for work," to "Work should be an exciting, fulfilling way to provide for myself and the people I care about." He had reprioritized his beliefs in this order: (1) self-actualization, followed by (2) family, (3) job satisfaction, and (4) money.

The fact that money was not the driving force behind his business strategy was, he recognized, an important detail of which anyone who worked with or for him should be aware. He eventually shared his beliefs with his new team and used them to lay down some ground rules. Everyone has to treat each other with integrity and respect; they are accountable for their behavior; and while results are important, there is no substitute for personal growth and self-discovery.

LIVING OUR BELIEFS

"Do you believe in reincarnation?" The question came from the fourth row. Fourteen heads turned in my direction, like sunflowers to the light. I was interested in the answer myself. In all my years in practice, this question was a first. What did I believe?

Spirituality and religious faith are not subjects I generally address in my work as a psychologist. And I'm not the only one. Psychotherapy has been late to understand the significance of the sacred and most therapists and counselors have been reluctant to approach it.[33] But an assignment in India forced me to look at the role religious belief plays in our personal and professional lives.

My first clue that religious belief was of great importance in the Indian workplace was the small framed photo most leaders had on their desk. The photos were strikingly similar—a black and white snapshot of an elderly gentleman with kind eyes and a full beard, someone I took to be a grandparent. After noticing many of these I decided to ask about the significance of these pictures. I knew that in India extended families were more likely to live under one roof than in the West, but ubiquitous pictures of grandparents wasn't something I had expected, even in India. It turned out the picture wasn't of a parent, grandparent, or relative, but of the leaders' guru (which literally translates to "teacher" or "mentor"). However, despite the prominent role the guru played in these leaders' lives these spiritual teachers were also a source of considerable dissonance. Vijay was one such leader I worked with who was struggling to square the teachings of his guru—to be compassionate in all things—with the aggressive leadership he saw practiced at many levels in Microsoft and which he felt were expected of him. I found Vijay to be a fascinating blend of humility, humor, and ambition and advised him that what he needed to move forward was to find his own brand of compassionate leadership, one that embraced his guru's truths and his own personal beliefs. (We shall see in the following chapter how creating a false self, which is what Vijay would have to do by choosing the expectations of the company over his beliefs, saps confidence and self-esteem).

Subsequent to working in India I took on a new client in the United States who, it turned out, was a practicing Christian. Unlike the leaders in India, who were not prohibited by corporate rules from sharing their religious beliefs, Human Resources had discouraged him from talking about his faith with coworkers, nor could he have any obvious religious imagery in his office. He seemed almost apologetic when talking to me about the tug-of-war between the secular expectations of the corporate world and his belief that his faith had to inform everything he did and said. We're still working to find a way for him to excel, to lead and still be true to himself. I mention him because his case reveals an unfortunate truth: Holding true to a strong set of beliefs often makes one's path harder, not easier.

Back to my own beliefs. Do I believe in reincarnation? I began to give a very analytical, academic nonanswer citing the scientific unlikelihood of reincarnation when I stopped myself. Why was I hiding my beliefs behind research and statistics? Why not just answer the damn question? I looked down at the pendant that I always wear around my neck. It's a Hebrew prayer inscribed on a piece of bone. Jewish children in Jerusalem used to wear these prayers pinned to the inside of their coats, keeping them safe but hidden from people who might be anti-Semitic. I'm not Jewish, but the piece reminds me to pay attention to the often neglected spiritual side of my life. As a psychologist, it's very easy to lose myself in the pain and suffering of my clients as well as the day-to-day intensity of the corporate world. This pendant is my own piece of spiritual armor, protecting me from losing my spiritual balance. And that's how I answered the question. I talked about the pendent and why it's important to me. I also explained that while I have no reason to believe in reincarnation I have my own set of spiritual beliefs that provide me comfort and allow me to stay strong. On this day, I learned far more about my own beliefs than probably anyone else in the room.

CLIMB THE RIGHT WALL

Joseph Campbell, the American writer on mythology, symbolism, and comparative religion, noted that many individuals have "gotten to the top of the ladder and found that it is against the wrong wall."[34] I've worked with a number of people in Microsoft who have gotten to the top of the ladder, only to experience a sense of emptiness or frustration. In Campbell's parlance, the "wall" they climbed was either externally driven or the result of faulty beliefs. That's why, preferably even before you start climbing your ladder, it's important:

- To identify what is important to you;
- to learn from experience;
- to integrate new learning into your beliefs and not be afraid to change your thinking;
- to seek meaning in adversity; and
- to not compromise what you believe in.

Leaders who embrace these actions climb their ladders faster, more effectively, and with more support, encouragement, and participation from those around them than leaders who don't. In addition, they are better able to cope with the unexpected pressures and surprises that great success brings.

Keep in mind this freeing concept: Who you are at work is who you are outside of work. While you shouldn't bulldoze your personal beliefs over the people you work with, you must act on your beliefs and live by them, or you will be plagued by self-doubt and ineffectiveness. You'll find that identifying and living according to your beliefs will be one of the most liberating things you've ever done.

Identifying your beliefs and then communicating them to everyone you work with are moments of truth for you and your business. How you interpret your life experiences and express your plans for the future are crucial in getting people to believe in your aspirations, ideas, or strategy. After all, if you don't believe in yourself and what you believe in, how can you expect others to believe in you?

BELIEFS: THINGS TO THINK ABOUT

Beliefs refresh: Beliefs are at the very heart of what makes us unique. They make me "me" and you "you." Beliefs stem from our life experiences, particularly our turning points—those events that have forced us to make choices that not only changed the course of our future but revealed what we really care about. The beliefs molded by these turning points shape our perceptions if the world, influencing how we make decisions, what we focus on, and what we ignore.

The following ten questions will help you learn more about your beliefs and provide guidelines to driving beliefs in to the heart of your business.

1. Do you have a set of clearly identified beliefs that guide your business and your behavior? If yes, what are they and what were the turning points that revealed them? If no, consider the following questions.

    a. List no more than three significant turning points in your life, situations where you had to make a decision that changed the course of your future and revealed what you really care about. Why were these three particularly significant to you? What decisions did they force you to make? What did you learn about yourself in making these decisions? What did you learn about other people? Did these experiences challenge any of your previously held beliefs?

    b. Based on these turning points list no more than five beliefs, beginning each time with the phrase, "As a leader I believe that . . ."

2. Which turning point best articulates your beliefs? Write a story that describes the event in detail and reveals the profound effect it had on you. How might this story help others you work with or lead them to understand more about you and what you want for your business?

3. Find opportunities to share your story with someone you work with. If you are able, tell your story at a team meeting or incorporate it into a presentation.

4. You want to drive beliefs into the core of your business. Call a meeting to explain to your team why beliefs are important. Share yours, and use a story to illustrate why they matter and how they affect the way you do business. Ask everyone whether they believe you will win in the marketplace given current conditions. If the overall reply is yes, head and heart are in alignment. If no, find out why—and what you and your team need to do to change this perception.

5. Have there been situations in which you compromised your beliefs? How did this affect the business? Looking back, what might you have done differently?

6. Invite your team to complete steps 1 and 2 above and ask them to share their answers.

   a. How are their beliefs similar to or different from yours and each other's?

   b. How might these beliefs impact the business going forward?

   c. Does a greater understanding of your team's beliefs require you to rethink at your strategy?

7. Do your beliefs get people out of bed in the morning, passionate and ready to change the world, or do they "keep people awake at night" causing anxiety, pressure, and doubt?

8. Based on your beliefs, what is your personal brand? Have you clearly established it within your organization? What could you do

to make your brand clearer to your coworkers? How can you incorporate this brand more explicitly into your work?

9. Is your company or business life event–prone? Do you think you experience more corporate life events than the average? Microsoft employees experience approximately 13 corporate life events per year. These include changes in strategy, launch of a new product or service, and changes in team structure. If you are experiencing the same or more events than Microsoft you are life event–prone. How can you communicate your beliefs more consistently and use them to help people in your business cope with the turmoil of repeated change?

10. Do you think your people have been scarred by repeated change or ambiguity (taking fewer risks, less confident about the future) or steeled by it (optimistic, believing in the necessity for change, and able to tell the story to their directs)?

3

Confidence

Why We Need It, How We Lose It,
How to Get It Back

Confidence influences the willingness to invest—to commit money, time, reputation, emotional energy, or other resources—or to withhold or hedge investment. This investment, or its absence, shapes the ability to perform. In that sense, confidence lies at the heart of civilization. Everything about an economy, a society, an organization, or a team depends on it.

—Rosabeth Moss Kanter, *Confidence: How Winning Streaks and Losing Streaks Begin and End*

Joanne was a tough lady. She ran an effective, responsive team, she was assertive, and she delivered results. She had always been supremely confident at work, until recently. Steve Ballmer and Bill Gates had taken a special interest in one of her projects, and consequently wanted to meet with her once a week for updates. Yet whenever she stood in front of these two corporate giants all her confidence would go out the window. She couldn't concentrate on her material and she'd stumble over her carefully crafted words. Fearing her poor presentations gave the impression that she was unprepared and inept, she came to me for help.

In our first session Joanne revealed that her confidence was first shaken during her very first meeting with the executives, when they had harshly challenged her presentation and questioned her recommendations. Since then, before every meeting with them, she'd engage in Fortune Telling[1]—a cognitive distortion in which we predict the negative outcome of an event based on the negative outcome of a past experience or event. In Joanne's mind, one meeting with Gates and Ballmer had gone badly, therefore every meeting she'd have with them would turn out badly. Essentially, she'd prepare herself to fail before she walked through the door.

Even the most capable leader like Joanne can come across a person or situation that suddenly opens a floodgate of self-doubt. Others suffer a general lack of confidence that weakens them like a low-grade flu. Whether episodic or chronic, low confidence can hamstring us professionally. In this chapter I define confidence, identify the six most common confidence traps, and reveal what we can do to get our confidence back.

WHAT IS CONFIDENCE?

In chapter 2 we talked about how our beliefs establish who we are and what we stand for. We can have many sets of beliefs, some of which affect how we perceive the world, some which affect how we perceive ourselves. Those self-beliefs are particularly key to our confidence. To be confident, we have to believe in others, but even more importantly, we have to believe in ourselves. In her book *Confidence*,[2] Rosabeth Moss Kanter, Professor of Business Administration at Harvard, writes, "Every step we take . . . is based on whether we feel we can count on ourselves and others to accomplish what has been promised. Confidence determines whether our steps—individually or collectivity—are tiny and tentative or big and bold."

Despite the importance of confidence as a construct, psychologists rarely talk about it, preferring instead to use terms such as self-esteem or optimism. They are not the same thing. Rather, they are the ingredients of confidence. We can therefore define confidence using the following formula[3]:

$$\text{Confidence} = \text{self belief} + \text{optimism} \times \text{importance}$$

I define confidence as the belief a person has that he or she can be successful in reaching a particular goal or objective, or accomplishing a certain task. Confidence only comes into play when we have something at stake, when a specific outcome matters to us. For example, if I am making an important presentation to a client to win new business, I am deeply invested in being successful and I need all the confidence I can get. If I am an observer in the same meeting, listening to the pitch, my level of confidence isn't relevant. I can sit back and relax because I have nothing at stake in the outcome.

Conversely, self-esteem is how we feel about ourselves 24/7—the emotional judgment we make about ourselves. I may not need confidence to observe the meeting, but my level of self-esteem will determine whether I feel that I deserve to be at the meeting. A psychologist might determine the strength of a person's self-esteem by asking, "On the whole, are you satisfied with yourself?" "All in all, are

83

you inclined to feel that you are a failure?" "Can you list a number of your good qualities?"

The two concepts are related. If we accomplish our goals the resulting confidence can improve our self-esteem. If we have low self-esteem it will impact how we approach a task. It's important when I meet a client who complains of feeling like a failure that I determine whether I am dealing with a confidence problem or a problem with low self-esteem; is it about a person's relationship with the self (self-esteem) or with achievement (confidence)?

DIAGNOSING CONFIDENCE PROBLEMS

When a new client comes to me for help with confidence problems, I go through my own series of questions to determine whether I am dealing with a confidence or self-esteem issue. I first probe for the strength of a client's self-beliefs. Does he see himself as a victim of circumstances? Does he dismiss his success as a lucky break, but attribute failure or setbacks to his own shortcomings and ineffectiveness? Does he see the glass as half empty? If the answers to these questions are *yes* then I can be reasonably certain he is struggling with low confidence. Conversely, during the course of our conversation it may become apparent that my client is struggling with unreasonable or unrealistic expectations. This client experiences a huge gap between who he is and who he aspires to be (his ideal self). This negative self-evaluation causes what psychologists call self-rejection. This person is very dissatisfied and critical of himself, and feels like a failure, with a cluster of symptoms that cause considerable anxiety and low self-esteem. In such cases my job isn't to boost my client's self-confidence, but rather to help him recalibrate his expectations, bringing the ideal closer to his current capabilities. Doing so helps create self-acceptance and a healthier, more robust sense of self-esteem. This may mean getting the client to reframe his ambitions. For example, many people can become frustrated if they don't move through the ranks quickly enough because they believe they are much better at their job than they actually are. Perhaps they have been told they need to stay in their current role a little longer to demonstrate the qualities required of a senior leader. This feedback does not accord with their view of where they believe they should be and causes self-rejection. Other clients find themselves living out a parent's fantasy and need to come to terms with their own aspirations and ideals.

I shadow my clients who exhibit low self-confidence and take note of whether they exhibit any of the core characteristics of confident people. Are they persistent? Can they be flexible? Are they optimistic? Are they capable of divergent thinking—that is, can they generate several solutions to a problem? Do they have a sense of control? I'll also ask their peers to complete the 360 assessment, which measures among other things the following behavioral indicators:

- They express confidence that goals will be achieved.
- They avoid sensitive, confrontational, or difficult topics.
- They become defensive, critical, or closed when given feedback.
- They stand up for their ideas even if they are unpopular.
- They display conviction, belief, and authenticity in their leadership role.
- They show persistence and tenacity in the face of adversity or resistance.

If my observations or the 360 ratings reveal low scores for these hallmarks of confident leadership, then I need to determine whether my client is suffering from a chronic problem or one that is situation specific.

IDENTIFYING THREATS TO OUR CONFIDENCE

Leaders struggling with low confidence have generally fallen prey to one of two enemies: an inner critic that derails their performance in specific situations, or a confidence trap that diminishes their self-belief and optimism all the time.

The Critic

Your mind is constantly chattering away, evaluating your performance, offering advice and interpreting events going on around you. Psychologists call this "self-talk," and it's perfectly normal. Ideally, our self-talk is like a coach—boosting our morale, helping us keep our perspective, psyching us up, and giving us comfort in unfamiliar surroundings. However, in certain situations, for example when we feel threatened, vulnerable, or judged, self-talk can turn ugly. Advice is replaced by criticism, optimism gives way to pessimism, hope fades and cynicism takes its place. In this case our self-talk becomes a critic—scolding us, comparing us to an impossible ideal, wearing down our confidence. Usually this negativity is short-lived, but for people already susceptible to pessimism, these negative thoughts can become an automatic response to life, translating every situation into a threat, silently gnawing away at their feelings of self-worth.

Take Bob, for example. When Bob's business reorganizes, he is promoted and given more responsibility. Part of his new role is to lead a product group, something he's never done before. As he drives to work in the morning, his inner critic starts in on him. "I'm lucky to get this job. They could have given it to Abby. She would have been better suited for it. I know I'm going to have a problem with the Product guys. I always do. I should have stayed where I was. I'll never be successful in this role. Everyone thinks I'm going to fail." Bob's internal monologue is full of emotionally loaded words and labels ("fail," "never be successful"), faulty assumptions ("I'm going to have a problem," "lucky to get this job"), and guilt-inducing statements ("I should"). He is evaluating his situation in a negative way, reframing his challenge and opportunity as a threat.

Bob is actually a client of mine. By the time we met, Bob had given so much ground to his inner critic that he didn't even realize that he approached the world in a negative, fearful way. With the help of Short Term Corporate Therapy, he fired his inner critic and hired the coach. The coach reframed Bob's internal monologue with a new kind of self-talk, one that sounded more like this. He would say, "I know I'm not going to fail—I got this new position because I deserve it. The Product group won't be a problem. Yes, we've tussled in the past, but I've always worked things out with them. I'll set up a meeting with the team to plan our next steps so I know everyone is on the same page." Practicing this revised self-talk improved Bob's mood and motivation, allowing him to see his promotion in a more positive light. It also propelled him beyond his fear so he could communicate openly with the product group and find ways to accelerate their integration into the larger team. Positive thinking—the coach—can't directly affect what happens to us, but it can directly affect the way we choose to address our problems, increasing the likelihood that we will, in fact, succeed.

A Critic Is Born

Identifying the origins of one's inner critic isn't always easy, but there is a formula we can use. It's called A, B, C. A refers to the antecedent— the situation that causes the critic to emerge. B is the behavior that affects how we think and feel, and C is the resulting action or consequence. My work with Nikolas reveals how we can use the A, B, C format to "out" our critic and be more effective.

Nikolas ran the sales division responsible for some of Microsoft's top European accounts. His team was distributed across some of Europe's major cities and had been hired because they were independent thinkers and could manage their businesses with a minimum of supervision. Nikolas had been asked to see me by his manager, with whom I had previously worked, who thought I could help Nikolas lead his team more effectively. I was warned he was becoming a micromanager of the worst kind. We started our work together with a 360 assessment. The data revealed Nikolas hoarded information and rarely involved his team in decision making. He refused to delegate, loading the most important assignments on his own shoulders. Shutting out the team made them feel he lacked confidence in them and they complained of feeling disempowered and lacking any positive connection with their boss. When we discussed the results, Nikolas confided that he did trust the team, but ceding control over important projects made him feel anxious. Based on our discussion and the verbatim feedback from his 360 I suspected the root cause of his problems to be a lack of self-confidence. I asked him to keep a diary for a few days so I might test out my hunch. In the diary he was to identify situations that threatened his self-confidence and to make a note of how he felt during these situations.

After a week, we reviewed his diary. We identified that the antecedents of the critic were situations in which he felt out of control. On one occasion, Nikolas wrote that he felt "dependent" and "paralyzed with fear" when he had to rely on two colleagues to contact him about a report they were compiling (the antecedent), which caused him to stall (the behavior), making it difficult to meet his commitments and deadlines (the consequence). His self-talk revealed a pattern of "magnification," where he exaggerated the problems caused by not being in control and minimized his ability to cope, and "emotional reasoning"—assuming his negative emotions reflect the way things really are.

Reading his thoughts and behaviors in black and white forced Nikolas to acknowledge how his lack of confidence in himself and others was fueling his need for control. Replacing his critic with a coach would help him think through his feelings, stop him from responding emotionally to situations where he felt out of control, and enable him to become more adaptable when faced with surprises. We also developed a mental picture he could turn to when he began to feel his inner critic stir. Nikolas said that he was often moved by a picture he had at home of a church on a rock surrounded by crashing waves. I asked him if there were any words he associated with the church that might reflect how he'd like to be perceived at work. He said the church was "authentic," "solid," and had "its own light." These phrases became his affirmations.

Beating the Inner Critic

To beat the critic, you have to know when he's most likely to rear his ugly head. That means identifying the situations that make you feel tense or worried, and then taking note of your internal monologue when you're in those situations. If you find that your self-talk is littered with phrases like, "I'll never be successful," "This always happens to me," or "I'm just not good enough," you need to change your thinking.

Joanne is a good example of how a person can root out their inner critic and change the way they think. We've established that Joanne's problem was episodic—her confidence was shaken only when she knew she had to face Bill Gates and Steve Ballmer. But why? In Joanne's defense, it isn't unusual for people to come away from a meeting with Gates and Ballmer feeling a little bruised. Many experience an emotional hangover for a day or two, but then they regain their confidence and get back on track.

So the first thing I wanted to know was what made Joanne so unusually vulnerable to the executives' feedback. I discovered it was very important to her to impress and get approval from "significant others" in her life. Psychologist Harry Stack Sullivan first referred to significant others in the 1950s to describe any person or group who has a strong influence on an individual's self-confidence.[4] If you work at Microsoft, there's no more significant other than Gates and Ballmer. To help Joanne gag her critic she had to stop Fortune Telling—predicting that her meetings with these two executives would turn out badly. We had to reduce the influence of these significant others and put her in back in touch with her confidence and competence, with the behaviors and attitude that had enabled her to become a senior leader in the first place.

To do this I asked her to describe what she felt like in situations where she was powerful and in control. As she spoke, I made notes of the descriptors she used: "grounded"; "strong"; "immovable." I then asked her if anything came to mind that exemplified these attributes.

She quickly mentioned a TV commercial that featured an insurance company whose logo is a rock jutting out of the sea, the Rock of Gibraltar. Over the centuries this island, located off the shore of Spain, has proved impervious to attack[5] and has inspired the simile "as solid as the Rock of Gibraltar" to describe a person who does not fail or a situation that cannot be overcome. We decided that the next time Joanne had a meeting with Gates or Ballmer, she would visualize the Rock of Gibraltar before entering the room, and repeat the words she had used to describe herself when she felt powerful and in control. By practicing this visualization and her "power" words she was able to replace her tendency to engage in Fortune Telling with healthy, adaptive self-talk. For example, instead of "They're going to bulldoze over me," she'd think, "I can stand my ground, I have something valuable to say." Instead of "I'm going to look stupid," she'd think, "They're not trying to trip me up or make me look foolish; they just want to know more about my thought process." This cognitive restructuring works because of the way our brain processes information. Unlike the computers many of us use every day our brains cannot consciously multitask. Despite what people may think, we cannot give our full attention to two things at once. It is not possible to read e-mail and simultaneously focus on what a colleague is saying, nor can we understand when several people talk at once. Similarly, the coach and the critic can't "talk" at the same time.

Cognitive therapy exploits this fact. Joanne couldn't engage in Fortune Telling if she focused instead on using her "power words." By allowing her coach to speak she silences the critic. To reprogram her thinking I asked her to put a picture of the Rock of Gibraltar on her desktop computer. Whenever she sees the image it reminds her to mentally rehearse more positive ways of thinking.

Keeping a diary is also a useful tool we can use to silence the inner critic. Not only does it provide important information I can use to help resolve my client's problem—for example, which situations cause the critic to emerge, what is at stake, and what the critic says—but it's also a useful device to increase a client's self-awareness. By focusing on the A, B, and C clients become more aware of how their self-talk is making them doubt themselves and lose confidence. The questions I ask them to answer in the diary vary, but most often I ask clients to use the "three column technique." In the first column they identify the situations that provoke the inner critic; in the second they record the types of twisted thinking they experience; and in the third they write down how it affects their behavior and the consequences of this behavior.

To help my clients identify the types of twisted thinking that accompany the critic I ask them to review the following list developed by psychiatrist David Burns.[6]

1. ALL-OR-NOTHING THINKING: You see things in black-or-white categories. If a situation is anything less than perfect, you see yourself as a total failure.

2. OVERGENERALIZATION: By using the words "always" or "never" you see a single event as a never-ending pattern of defeat.

3. MENTAL FILTER: You pick out a single negative detail and dwell on it. No matter how much praise you receive, all that registers is the one word of criticism.

4. DISCOUNTING THE POSITIVE: You reject positive experiences by insisting they don't count. If you do a good job you tell yourself you were just lucky or that anyone could have done as well.

5. JUMPING TO CONCLUSIONS: You interpret things negatively when there are no facts to support your conclusion. Two common

variations are mind-reading (you arbitrarily conclude that someone in the meeting is reacting negatively to you) and fortune-telling (you assume and predict that the meeting will turn out badly).

6. MAGNIFICATION: You exaggerate the importance of your problems and shortcomings, or you minimize your desirable qualities.

7. EMOTIONAL REASONING: You assume that your negative emotions reflect the way things really are: "I feel guilty. I must be a terrible person."

8. SHOULD STATEMENTS: You tell yourself that things should be the way you hoped or expected them to be.

9. LABELING: An extreme form of all-or-nothing thinking. Instead of saying, "I made a mistake," you attach a negative label to yourself: "I'm no good." Once ascribed to a person, labels are very, very difficult to shift.

10. PERSONALIZATION AND BLAME: You hold yourself personally responsible for events that aren't entirely under your control.

If clients find it hard to remember to "check in" with their thoughts, I ask them to purchase a sheet of small self-adhesive red dots from an office supply store. They place the dots on items that they use on a daily basis, for example, the lid of their laptop, a notebook, inside a purse or wallet, or on the side of their computer monitor. The key is to put the dots in places that they will notice over the course of a day and that, when they see them, will remind them to listen to their thoughts and pay attention to their feelings.

If someone's critic is particularly loud and insistent, I advise her to try wearing a rubber band around her wrist. Every time she starts to hear the critic, she is to snap the band against her wrist. The pain reminds her to shift her focus onto more positive thoughts and imagery.

CONFIDENCE TRAPS

The inner critic, as damaging as it can be, generally only weakens a person's self-confidence in certain situations. But some people fall into confidence traps that undermine their feelings of effectiveness to such an extent that there is little in their life that isn't touched by it. Anything that continually sabotages your belief in your ability to achieve is a confidence trap. These habits of thinking and behaving are very hard to break as they may have guided our behavior for many years. There are six traps that seem to affect leaders the most.

Trap 1: Fear of failure
Trap 2: Fear of success
Trap 3: Overfunctioning
Trap 4: The false self
Trap 5: The impostor syndrome
Trap 6: Shoulds and shouldn'ts

All of these traps have a common cause; a dysfunctional relationship with success. What differentiates them is the thinking and behavior that accompanies each.

Trap #1: Fear of Failure

In its classic form leaders who suffer from a fear of failure (FOF) desperately want to succeed but the fear associated with failing is so great they prefer not to try at all. The self-talk that destroys their confidence is grounded in "overgeneralization," a self-belief that communicates, "If I fail at this I will fail at everything."

This type of negative thinking impacts leaders' interpersonal relationships. They often jump to conclusions, fearing that if things don't
go well they will lose people's respect and approval. The fear of social
rejection, or of not measuring up, plays a big part in FOF and is
closely aligned with another trap, Imposter Syndrome, which I discuss in a later section. In his account of the rise of the sports channel
ESPN, Mike Freeman writes about how co-host Keith Olbermann
became a nightmare to work with, haranguing colleagues and on
more than one occasion driving coworkers to tears.[7] Olbermann, it
turned out, had a chronic fear of failure. His fear was driven by a
belief that he was responsible for events that were outside of his
control—a type of twisted thinking called "personalization." He'd try
to overcompensate for his feelings of inadequacy by taking on the role
of Superman, stepping in to fix whatever threatened to go awry.
Unfortunately this strategy backfired as Olbermann developed a
"dread of being blamed for things going wrong." In an apology written to his coworkers after the publication of Freeman's book,
Olbermann attributed his behavior to his deep-seated insecurity. He
confided, "I've always believed everyone around me was more qualified and competent, and I wasn't, and that some day I'd be found
out." There is no doubt that in most people's eyes Olbermann was
successful, yet he lived in fear and self-loathing. His fear eventually
forced him to leave his job.

The origins of FOF lie in dysfunctional parenting. Children high
in FOF often have mothers who punish failure but react neutrally to
success. These children tend to have an insecure attachment to their
parents, characterized by a fear of rejection and disapproval. I
discuss the implications of different attachment styles further in
chapter 4.

Trap #2: Fear of Success

Freud was one of the first to recognize that people could be "wrecked by success,"[8] observing that, "People occasionally fall ill precisely because a deeply rooted and long cherished wish has come to fulfillment."

It may seem strange to think that some people fear success but it can and does affect many individuals. There are several possible causes of FOS. One is a lack of confidence that causes people to dread the aftermath of success. What if they succeed? What then? Success will raise everyone's expectations, but what if they can't do a repeat performance? They attribute success to luck or chance and not to their best efforts. Another cause of FOS may be gender identity. Some studies suggest that women are more vulnerable to Fear of Success because they often experience a conflict between their achievements and their role as women, a conflict caused by gender role stereotyping. Competition, achievement, and drive are appropriate and attractive qualities for a man but unattractive attributes for a woman. She may sabotage or avoid success because she fears she will lose her femininity by becoming one of the boys.[9]

When those with FOS do achieve their goals, they often become ill or suffer from severe emotional problems such as anxiety. Someone who is constantly sick could very well be looking for a way to gracefully exit a situation that has become unbearable. For example, I once met a phenomenal athlete who had developed a mystery illness that prevented her from competing on the circuit. It started with a cold and sniffles, but as time went by her health never improved. When we met I was full of sympathy, imagining she was heartbroken to miss out on competitions for which she had trained so hard. So I was surprised to learn she regarded her enforced absence as a good thing. By staying sick she was off the hook; she no longer had to fear disappointing her parents. This type of avoidant behavior can also play out in the organization. Ill health can be a way the success-phobic executive can beat a socially acceptable retreat from the pressures of the job.

Trap # 3: Overfunctioning

People who overfunction lack confidence in their ability to manage relationships. Deep down they have little belief in themselves or their ability to manage the people they lead. Overfunctioners have a hard time delegating, thus preventing others from challenging themselves, meeting their personal goals, and finding fulfillment in their work. In its extreme form, an overdeveloped sense of responsibility creates a codependent relationship between the leader and his directs, who often underfunction in response to their overfunctioning leader. In its extreme form team members become so dependent on the leader that if they leave to take another job the team implodes and becomes incapable of functioning.

A person who overfunctions might[10]:

- Give advice even if it isn't wanted;
- do things for others they could and should do for themselves;
- worry about others;
- feel responsible for others and think they know what is best for them;
- talk more than listen;
- have goals for others they do not have for themselves; and
- experience periodic, sudden burnouts.

Sofia's story is an excellent example of the cost and cause of overfunctioning. Sofia had recently been promoted to run a small cross-functional team operating out of the Netherlands. She felt she'd been pushed into the deep end of the pool, unable to cope with the demands of her new role. Her lack of confidence prevented her from asking for help from her manager. She felt she had to go it alone to prove herself. She and I initially met to debrief a leadership survey she had completed, but during our meeting it became clear that she was unhappy in her work and was finding it increasingly difficult to manage the different roles in her life—manager, wife, and mother. To cope with the role strain, she was overfunctioning at work and underfunctioning at home.

Role strain is a fairly common problem and occurs where there is a conflict in fulfilling the different expectations associated with a person's different roles in life. For example, a leader's role in many big companies might require him to work late and on weekends. This conflicts with his role as partner or parent. In some cases it results in significant cognitive dissonance when the person feels he cannot fulfill any role well, leading to feelings of anxiety and hopelessness, and overfunctioning behavior.

If I suspect role strain I ask my client to draw two faces on a whiteboard or piece of paper. One is their self at work, the other their self at home. Then we analyze the drawings to identify any differences between the two roles. Sophia portrayed her work self as a mother figure, breast-feeding several babies (see Figure 3.1). Her drawing of her home self showed two figures—herself and her husband. He was holding her while she cried because she had no more to give to him, depleted after a long day looking after her "work children." As we talked through the drawing we discussed what could be driving her behavior. Overfunctioning is often caused by anxiety, so I asked her about job stress and her feelings of confidence. She explained she had

Figure 3.1

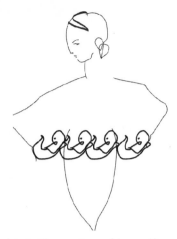

Sophia's illustration of herself at work.

Sophia's illustration of herself at home.

inherited a young team, one that was, in her opinion, relatively inexperienced, whose ability to do the job she did not fully trust. This is why she felt the need to overfunction—she was afraid of the consequences should she leave them on their own. This was not the full story, however. She also confessed to a lack of belief in her own abilities to be successful, so in addition to not fully trusting her team, she didn't trust herself. We discussed various ways she could change the system she had created—empowering her direct reports by becoming less hands-on, tackling her low confidence by examining the thoughts and feelings she had about her own effectiveness. One particular issue she had to overcome was the inability to say no to her boss. As one of her directs commented, "She is very eager to please the people above her and the people under her often has [*sic*] to pay for that, since it creates a stressed environment and very big work load for the teams. Can't she say no to the people above her?" To conquer this particular problem we worked on her interpersonal style, helping her realize that she was being passive in her relationships with others. In her misguided effort to please her boss she was destroying not just her own confidence, but also her boss' confidence in her. She had to become much more assertive and learn to believe in herself and those who worked for her. To achieve this she kept a diary of her interpersonal style (I say more about this concept in chapter 4), and the thoughts and feelings she experienced in her relationships with her boss and subordinates. This way she became more aware as to how her choice of style impacted her effectiveness and confidence.

Trap 4: The False Self

Donald Winnicot, the British pediatrician and psychoanalyst, introduced the concept of "True Self" and "False Self" into the taxonomy of psychoanalysis in the 1960s.[11] He positioned the True Self as the integrated, healthy, confident self that we are born to be. The False Self is a construction that starts early on in life as a means of pleasing one's parents. Children will follow the rules and behave in accordance with their parents' values because that's what elicits praise and rewards. But as children grow and mature, they usually begin to question and challenge the rules and values they once accepted from their parents, leading to the almost universal teenage rebellion. What comes out on the other side (too many years later, some parents believe) are individuals who have acknowledged their True Self, and who balance what their parents taught them with revelations they have made on their own.

But that's certainly not the end of the False Self. At work, it's an often appropriate if not an unspoken requirement that we present a False Self that happily adapts to the norms and culture of the organization. We may not agree with everything the company stands for, or appreciate certain aspects of how our executives run our businesses, but usually we keep quiet about these things in the interest of getting along and getting the job done. Some people, however, feel they have to take their False Self to extremes. Deep down they feel that to be accepted and successful they have to create a front. Keeping up this False Self drains a person's confidence. These people become victims of their desire to fit in at any cost, like the hapless visitors to Procrustes' inn. This Greek myth tells of an innkeeper who kept a house by the side of the road where he offered hospitality to passing strangers, inviting them in for a pleasant meal and a night's rest in his very special bed. He promised that its length would exactly match whoever lay down upon it. What Procrustes didn't volunteer was the method by which this "one-size-fits-all" was achieved—namely, as soon as the guest lay down, Procrustes went to work, stretching him on the rack if he was too short for the bed and chopping off his legs if he was too long. A False Self forces people to stretch or censor parts of themselves so as to remain "safe" within their organization or team.

John was just such a case. A general manager, he ran energized teams that usually met their goals. He was well respected, though considered a little aloof, and from the outside seemed to be thriving at Microsoft. One day I was in a meeting when John knocked on the door and asked if he could see me immediately. Normally I would have been frustrated by this interruption, but he looked so tired and drawn I agreed to adjourn the meeting and follow him back to his office.

Once there, he revealed that he had been suffering from severe anxiety in the mornings while getting ready for work. That day he was suffering from a panic attack that wouldn't subside. I asked him what he was thinking about when he started to feel the anxiety in the morning, and he replied, "My suit of armor." Suit of armor? "The suit of armor I have to wear to protect myself." Against what, I asked. He couldn't immediately answer, but as we spoke that day and in sessions over the next few weeks, it became clear that John was staggering under the weight of a False Self.

He was the son of a perfectionist. His father was a professional sportsman and medical practitioner with high hopes for John in both fields. Over the course of his childhood, John rebelled against his father's wishes, giving up a promising sports career and turning to business rather than medicine. Yet despite these attempts at independence, John had not outgrown his father's expectations. He had just projected them onto Microsoft. John had forged a False Self to cope with his father's demands and he had now recreated it at work. His need for autonomy and independence was sublimated by a more compliant, cooperative persona and keeping up this False Self was smothering him. It also explained why his coworkers found him aloof. If your True Self becomes submerged by a False Self, no one can get to know you. You may not even get to know yourself.

Over the course of our sessions together John recognized that throughout his life he had made decisions based on what others wanted—in particular, his father and Microsoft—and it was time to make some decisions for himself, to figure out what he wanted to do. He subsequently left Microsoft to start his own company, one where he could be his True Self and build something that was all his own.

The False Self is a confidence trap that prevents us from realizing our true potential. We believe that who we are is not good enough, or does not measure up to some external bar or criteria set for us by others, so we censor it and create a more socially acceptable persona. This unhappiness with who we really are causes self-rejection and a corresponding drain on our feelings of self-confidence. How can we believe in our potential for success if we feel ashamed of who we are?

Trap 5: Impostor Syndrome

Mona was an impostor, or so she believed. Despite all evidence to the contrary—a successful career with several leading technology companies, awards and promotions at Microsoft—she lived in fear that people would figure out what she secretly thought was true, that her success could be chalked up to luck and a mentoring boss, not that she was good at her job. She had always been the teacher's pet in school, and she had continued to try to earn the approval of her superiors in the same way in her working life, developing an unswerving loyalty to her boss in an unspoken contract to be the favored employee. But as his business grew and other equally talented people came on board, she no longer felt special. The final straw was when her boss reorganized the group and decided that she should report to someone else. She interpreted this as a sign that she was dispensable, and it badly shook her confidence. Now she felt like just another cog in the wheel.

Mona exhibited two of the four classic characteristics of someone suffering from Impostor Syndrome, as outlined in psychotherapist Pauline Clance's book *The Imposter Phenomenon*.[12] (The other two are Fear of Failure and Discounting the Positive.)

1. She needed to be the best. Mona wasn't happy unless she received external affirmation that she was better—at her job, in this case—than other people around her. As children and adolescents individuals with IS are usually at or near the top of the class. They are, as the psychiatrist Bryan Lask remarks, "perfect" children, good at everything,

"easy-going, contented and cooperative."[13] They are more often girls than boys (IP affects more women than men) and have very high expectations of themselves academically, socially, and in sports and games. They cannot bear to fail at anything.

2. She was a perfectionist. In and of itself perfectionism is not a bad thing. Psychologist D. E. Hamachek suggests that both normal perfectionism and neurotic perfectionism exist.[14] "Normal" perfectionists set high but reasonable or realistic standards for themselves—what in Microsoft are often called stretch goals. "Neurotic" perfectionists tend to strive for excessively high standards and are motivated by a Fear of Failure and of disappointing others. There is little room in neurotic perfectionists' lives for reflection because they are too busy "doing" to slow down and ask themselves why they are doing it. Eventually, all they can see is what they haven't accomplished, dismissing their successes as irrelevant flukes.

Trap 6: Shoulds and Shouldn'ts

"You sound just like your mother." Words that strike fear and occasionally loathing into many adult children. And yet, for most of us, the only road map we have in raising our own children is the one provided by our own parents. They lay down many "scripts" that we act out as we grow and mature. Some of these scripts are useful; others can become barriers to our success and feelings of accomplishment. For example, parents who support and encourage their child's best efforts despite failure and setbacks help develop an adult who is self-directed and who has learned to enjoy the process as well as the goal. Conversely, parents who are impatient, who place their own needs above those of their child, who are overprotective and set unrealistic expectations, undermine their child's autonomy and feelings of competence.[15] Children from these types of families internalize scripts that send the message, "You will never succeed without our support. The world is a scary place and you cannot be trusted to cope with it on you own."

Some scripts become fossilized, hidden under the sediment of our life experiences only to be rediscovered at a turning point. Many contain "should" statements—"You should never lose a game," "You should always get the part"—tyrannical injunctions that can create strong feelings of guilt and shame, and considerable doubt in our abilities later on in life, if we don't feel we're living up to parental expectations. For example, children who are told they should always get straight As will feel incompetent as adults if they don't always have the right answers. As Matt McKay points out, "The fact is that many of the 'Should's' you grew up with simply don't apply any more. They don't fit you because they were created by your parents to fit their needs."[16] The problem is we unconsciously incorporate them into our adult life where they continue to guide our behavior and sap our self-confidence.

For example, Mike came to see me concerned that his team was upset because he controlled the decision-making process. They had also accused him of always having to have the last say. Over the course of our conversation I noticed that Mike spoke repeatedly about what the team "should be doing" differently. On a hunch, I asked him to write down what his parents had told him he should or shouldn't do when he was a small boy. He filled a couple of flip charts with his should and shouldn't list. One "should" that resonated with him was that he always "should finish everything on his plate." This didn't come as a surprise to me. Mike was a big man, and he admitted that he had long struggled with a weight problem caused by overeating. We talked about how his parents' food-related instruction could be playing out with his team. As with each plate of food, he felt compelled to finish each decision and have the last say. In doing so he was robbing his team of their confidence. Over the course of the next few sessions he worked on reducing the number of "should" statements he used with his team and made sure he gave them the opportunity to have the last word.

IS THERE SUCH A THING AS TOO MUCH CONFIDENCE?

We've spent a lot of time exploring the various ways in which low self-confidence can derail capable leaders. But then there are those people who seem to have a surfeit of confidence, the ones who seem to think they're smarter than everyone else, who take tremendous pride in their accomplishments and tend to take outside opinions or suggestions with a grain of salt. Obviously, these individuals are unlikely to seek me out. And certainly, their confidence seems to pay off. We often find these people in extreme positions of power, which might imply that a tremendous amount of confidence is desirable because these people usually get what they want, when they want it. One of the more interesting examples of the overconfident leader is Steve Jobs of Apple, who is famous for being able to sway people into believing "almost anything with a skillful mixture of charm, charisma, slight exaggeration, and clever marketing."[17] Another well-known leader whose confidence seems to know no bounds is Larry Ellison, the chief executive of Oracle. In his book on Ellison, Mike Wilson jokes, "What's the difference between God and Larry Ellison?" The answer? "God doesn't think he is Larry Ellison!"[18] Both Jobs and Ellison have used their abundant self-confidence to great effect. Apple and Oracle are very successful companies. But can too much confidence ever be a bad thing?

Recent studies have found that in some cases overconfidence can go hand-in-hand with narcissism, characterized by an abiding self-centeredness and an inflated view of one's ability to be successful.[19] And just how solid are an overconfident person's predictions of success? Keith Campbell found that when compared with "normal" controls, subjects who were identified as narcissistic "were found to be more overconfident" but that "these inflated ability estimates were not accompanied by greater ability." In fact, what Campbell found was that "Narcissists were found to [do less well] on a betting task, reflecting narcissists' greater overconfidence and willingness to place risky bets."[20] Moreover, in his study of narcissistic leaders psychoanalyst Michael Maccoby warns that these charismatic leaders "listen only for the kind of information they seek. They don't learn easily from others. They don't like to teach but prefer to indoctrinate and make speeches [and] they dominate meetings with subordinates."[21] That's quite a list! The executive who is narcissistic has a tough road ahead, for him and his business. While his personality might make it seem as though anything is possible, his judgment is not infallible. In fact, his inflated tendency to take risks can derail even the most successful company.

REGAINING SELF-CONFIDENCE

The number of people struggling with low self-confidence is vastly higher than the number of those suffering from too much, so the rest of this chapter addresses how we can get our confidence back when we've lost it.

Whether we're tackling episodic or chronic low self-confidence, the first thing to do is assess the form the problem takes—identify the trap we are caught in, the type of negative self-talk we use, and the degree of impairment the trap or inner critic imposes on our daily life. For example, do you regularly avoid situations that threaten your self-confidence, such as presenting your ideas to a large group or managing conflict between two of your employees? Do you overfunction in an effort to maintain confidence and control?

Second, how does such negative self-talk serve you? What are you able to avoid by staying in the trap? There is *always* a payoff to our self-destructive behavior, whether it's avoiding conflict, pleasing others, or becoming the popular and sympathetic colleague.

The following five questions can help you become more aware of how you may nurture the critic and lay your own traps.

1. Are there parts of my life I am refusing to acknowledge?
2. How do I make life difficult for myself?
3. How do I create fear in my life?
4. Am I blaming others for my situation?
5. How do I contribute to my own lack of confidence?

Third, you have to conduct a "surgical strike" on the harmful attitudes and beliefs you hold about yourself. Much has been written about how leaders and managers need to become less emotionally constipated and more emotionally intelligent, more in touch with their feelings, and to acknowledge how their feelings can impact those around them. The pendulum, however, has swung too far in favor of the subjective. What we could all actually use is a heavy dose of objectivity. The wholesale embrace of Emotional Intelligence places far too much emphasis on our feelings and not on the thoughts that cause them. The successful executive is the one who is able to balance EQ and IQ. Neither should dominate the other.

REALITY TESTING

There is a fairly simple way to become more objective about the cause of our problems. We can "scrub" our beliefs using a technique cognitive psychologists call Reality Testing.

Look at table 3.1. In column 1, note as many beliefs as you can about yourself. For example, you might write "I should always have the answer" or "It's not acceptable to say no." Once you identify your beliefs, take a good hard look at them. Are they reasonable? Are you demanding too much of yourself? By assessing your beliefs in black and white, you can begin to see how realistic or unrealistic they are. If

Table 3.1 Reality Test

Beliefs	Reasonable (R) or Unreasonable (U)	Changing Your Beliefs
People will find out that I'm really not as good as they think.	U	No one thinks I'm a fraud but me. I'm the one putting all the pressure on me. My manager gave me some great feedback—I need to focus on that. Also, I know I will make some mistakes but that doesn't mean I am a failure or a fraud.
I need this business pitch to be successful but I just know I am going to screw up. Maybe I should ask Bob to do it.	U	Looking at this objectively, what am I saying to myself here? I'm the best one for the job. If I practice the presentation and get some feedback from my colleagues, I'll feel more comfortable.

you continually put yourself under a lot of pressure with unrealistic expectations, your performance and enjoyment at work will decline and your feelings of confidence will drop. In column 2, put an R if you think the belief is reasonable, or a U if the belief is unreasonable, even impossible to live up to. In the final column, try to reframe your unrealistic beliefs so that they are motivational and not demoralizing.

By writing your beliefs down in this fashion you can begin to regain control to escape whatever confidence trap you are in. Keeping a diary and using the three-column technique are also exercises you can use to recognize your twisted thinking for yourself. Seeing these crooked thoughts in black and white is the first step to changing them. As I tell my clients, the first thing to do if you are in a confidence trap is to stop digging! We won't stop digging our trap if we focus solely on how we feel. Only by identifying the thoughts that cause our lack of confidence can we change our self talk and adopt a more positive attitude.

CONFIDENCE AND ITS EFFECTS ON OTHERS

As a leader it's important to realize that confidence doesn't just affect your performance, it affects the performance of those you lead. The mechanism by which this happens is termed emotional contagion. You probably work with or know someone who is high-strung, anxious, and fidgety. How do you feel after a short time in his company? High-strung, anxious, and fidgety? This is an example of emotional contagion—the process by which we "catch" each others' emotions.[22] It's surely no surprise that recent research has shown people are susceptible to the moods of others, whether by mimicking someone else's facial expressions and vocalizations, or simply feeling good in someone else's presence. Upon meeting President Roosevelt, Winston Churchill said, "His buoyant sparkle, his iridescence, was like opening a bottle of champagne."[23] Roosevelt was known for having utter faith in himself and his country and this unbridled confidence had a corresponding positive effect on those around him. The process is described in a terrific article called "Mimic Your Way to the Top": "Here's the scene: the top executives of Microsoft Corp. are in a meeting and cofounder and CEO Bill Gates is talking. As he grows intense he starts rocking and bobbing back and forth in his chair, the rocking and bobbing speeding up as he continues. Seated around him, several of his lieutenants soon are rocking and bobbing. Gates periodically pushes his glasses up on his nose; his associates push their glasses up."[24] Subordinates relentlessly copy their bosses' mannerisms, gestures, and ways of speaking. Such is the power of Bill Gates that his syntax has become part of the normal Microsoft vocabulary. People don't think, they "cycle"; going deep on a subject is "drilling down"; being analytical is "being granular"; being concise is "netting it out"; and "brainstorming" is "riffing on an idea." "Billspeak" provides an instant indicator of who is an insider (they know what these terms mean) and who is new or an outsider. This type of contagion is healthy as it provides employees with a sense of identity and belonging that is uniquely Microsoft. There are, however, situations where this contagion can be damaging. To make the distinction I explain to my clients that when it comes to confidence some leaders are radiators while others are drains.

RADIATORS AND DRAINS

A confident leader, like Roosevelt, is a *radiator*—someone who motivates and excites others, who is passionate, and who people want to listen to and be around. A leader plagued by self-doubt is a *drain*—generally negative, sapping our energy, and bleeding us dry. Drains are psychic vampires, leaving us exhausted and unmotivated.

One good example of a master radiator is Bill Gross, founder of Idealab, an Internet incubation company. During the dotcom boom Idealab burned through millions of venture capital funding start-ups like eToys and Petsmart.com. When boom turned to bust Icarus had his wings clipped by extravagant market capitalization that couldn't deliver. Gross had to let go of half the company's staff. Joe Nocera writes in the *New York Times*, "There was a lot of soul searching and anguish over the mistakes [Gross] made. But not for a minute did Mr. Gross think about liquidating Idealab."[25] That's because one of Gross's greatest strengths is his eternal optimism. Despite considerable setbacks he never lost his belief that his company could work. His belief wasn't unfounded—venture capitalists are again investing in Idealab, costs are under control, and the company is generating considerable excitement in the technology community.

A confident, optimistic leader provides hope to those around him or her. Rebecca Solnit, a cultural historian, writes, "All transformations begin in the imagination, in hope. To hope is to gamble. It's a bet on the future, on your desires, on the possibility that an open heart and uncertainty is better than gloom and safety."[26] She concludes, "To hope is dangerous, and yet it is the opposite of fear, for to live is to risk." The leader who has hope commits herself to the future; to being visible and accountable for what she believes in. This visibility enables others to believe all things are possible.

Perhaps one of the better-known contemporary radiators is Steve Ballmer, the CEO of Microsoft. His speeches are the stuff of legend and on stage he has the ability to lift thousands of employees and infuse them with his passion and energy. But how does he do it? Some people are indeed better "senders" of emotions. They display a rich nonverbal language and score highly on measures of extraversion—in other words, they exhibit behaviors commonly associated with confident people. Weak senders are far more introverted and less likely to exhibit nonverbal cues. Given this, it might be easy to conclude that successful leaders must be natural extroverts. Yet there is evidence that this is not necessarily the case. For example, despite his public persona, Richard Branson, the CEO of Virgin, claims to be an introvert. "Before we launched the airline, I was a shy and retiring individual who couldn't make speeches and get out there . . . I had to train myself into becoming more of an extrovert."[27] Ultimately, extroverts and introverts can succeed equally well; their talents and gifts are expressed differently, but no less effectively. What is indispensable to a successful leader, however, is a high level of confidence.

CONFIDENCE: THINGS TO THINK ABOUT

Confidence is the belief you have that you will be successful in reaching a goal or objective that is important to you. Leaders struggling with low self-confidence have fallen prey to one of two enemies: an inner critic that derails performance in specific situations, or a confidence trap that diminishes self-belief and optimism.

The following questions will help you identify whether you are a radiator or drain, and in the grip of the coach or critic.

1. In which situations is your confidence the strongest? Why is this? Are there things you can learn from this that you could transfer to other situations at work?

2. Do you approach new situations or important goals or objectives with can-do assurance or are there specific situations that impact your confidence and give rise to the critic? Which are they? What does your inner critic say to you? Use the ten types of twisted thinking I describe on pages 92–93 to help you.

3. Do you overfunction in order to control your relationships, going deep into someone's business without their knowledge or agreement? What might be the impact of this behavior on your subordinates? Why do you need to stay in this trap?

4. Give your beliefs a reality test. Write down your beliefs about yourself. How have they served you in getting you to this point in your life? Do they indicate that you have reasonable expectations of yourself or are you demanding too much? Are there any you can reframe so they are more reasonable?

5. Are there parts of yourself you censor when you come into work in the morning? What do you hide? Why might you do this? What do you fear might happen if you didn't censor this part of yourself?

6. Are you a radiator or a drain? Does your mood and behavior inspire and motivate or drain people of passion and commitment? What do you do to inspire others? How might you do more of this? What about others in your business—are there people you avoid because of their mood or temperament?

Self-Awareness and Your Behavioral Signature

"Leaders are people who are able to express themselves fully . . . The key to full self expression is understanding one's self and the world, and the key to understanding is learning—from one's own life and experience."[1]

How well do you know yourself? And how do you know what you know? These are the two key questions that must be answered in our quest for self-awareness—a warts-and-all assessment of our strengths and vulnerabilities. I have been on something of a crusade to improve all of my clients' self-awareness because it significantly correlates with their ability to lead effectively.

In chapter 1, we learned how our beliefs are shaped by the turning points in our lives, providing fertile material with which to identify the things that really matter to us. In chapter 2, we discussed how our family of origin can impact our confidence—for good and ill. It might seem that this chapter on self-awareness should be more of the same—keeping our focus inward, building our ability to reflect on, interpret, and absorb the implications of our personal history and our life experiences. Paradoxically, however, we're going to turn our gaze outward, because I define a self-aware leader as one who ultimately focuses less on himself and more on the impact he has on others.

In *Being and Nothingness* by French philosopher Jean-Paul Sartre, a man in a hotel peeks through a keyhole, his attention fully absorbed on what he can see in the room. "All of a sudden I hear footsteps in the hall. Someone is watching me." Now the voyeur's attention shifts away from what he can see in the room toward the person in the hallway, and he feels shame as he realizes what that person must be thinking. My point is this: When trying to get people to follow our lead, it doesn't matter what we do or how we do it. What matters is how they interpret what we do and how we do it. Being unaware of the effect we have on other people will undermine every move we make.

DIAGNOSING SELF-AWARENESS

In my experience people constantly overestimate their self-awareness. In fact, aggregating all the results from the 360s I have conducted with leaders and managers, of the forty-two items in the assessment, those relating to self-awareness rank lowest. There are many consequences associated with this statistic, the main one being that these leaders have little awareness of the impact they have on those around them. They could be winning hearts and minds or turning people off completely. The low scores also imply that many of us are so focused on the next meeting, presentation, or goal that we give no thought to why we behave the way we do, let alone whether the behavior is appropriate or not. The truth is we operate for much of the time on autopilot; it's only when things don't go the way we expected or someone doesn't behave as we'd predicted that we are forced take stock of how we might have contributed to the problem. Consider this example. Vikram worked out of the Canadian subsidiary. He had been on the fast track, but his career had stalled. I had spent many hours as his sounding board while he frantically reorganized his group over and over in an attempt to build the perfect high performance team that could help his business regain momentum. One day he came in and casually mentioned that he was thinking of "blowing up" his new team and starting from scratch. "Why?" I asked, "You've spent so much time and effort putting this team together." He said he wasn't sure it was the right thing to do, but anything would be better than the status quo. I found this nebulous reply unsatisfactory. He was so close to having everything he wanted, and now he was going to throw it away? Something didn't add up. I started asking him questions about his feelings toward stability and change, which one he preferred and why. Eventually he brought up his father—a senior lecturer at a prestigious Canadian university. Vikram explained that appearances were very important to his father, so with every promotion or raise he'd uproot the family and move them to a new and bigger house so that his colleagues and community would know about his heightened success. One move so taxed the family budget that they ate nothing but rice for six months. I asked Vikram if he saw any parallels between his behavior and his father's. He acknowledged that he, like his father, equated success with constant transformation and that he was forcing his team to "eat rice" in his quest for recognition and success. Vikram is a perfect example of someone who had low self-awareness, who was oblivious to the reasons for his behavior and the impact he was having on others.

117

I ask my clients three questions when diagnosing or gauging their level of self-awareness:

1. Are you aware of how your behavior impacts others and can you change it when necessary?
2. Do you actively seek out feedback from different sources regarding your strengths and weaknesses?
3. Can you listen to feedback or criticism without shutting down, becoming defensive, or lashing out at the messenger?

The first question points to where clients might focus their attention predominantly on themselves, on others, or, ideally, both. For example, Carl and I were coming to the end of our work together and I needed him to become much more aware of how his behavior affected others. It often happens that I get a lot of unsolicited feedback on the behavior of the leader I am working with from his or her directs, peers or colleagues and I had been getting a steady stream of feedback about Carl's behavior. There was no doubt he had made significant progress on identifying his beliefs and building his own brand, but as for "playing well with others" he was a bull in a china shop. We started our session together by talking about the notion of self-awareness and I introduced him to the cards I use with clients to help them reflect on their behavior (I first introduced the "cards as homework" concept in chapter 1). The idea is that a Leader takes one card a week at random from the pack and reflects on the question printed on the card. I gave Carl a pack and in typical fashion he immediately took the wrapper off and started looking at the questions. After a moment's pause he started to use the analogy of driving a car to describe becoming self-aware. "I need to become more aware of what all the knobs and dials do so I can drive more effectively," he observed. I loved the analogy but pointed out that I was less concerned with him learning about the inside of his car and more interested in how he was driving. I commented, "You're too focused on you Carl and ignoring the others on the road—are you a careful driver? Do you cut people off and frustrate other drivers on the road. Do you indicate and message your intentions?" He got my point. He then extended his "car analogy" to his directs by drawing a car and a camper on a sheet of paper. "The car is me," he said, "and the camper my directs. I'm doing all the driving and they could be up to anything—playing cards, sleeping. How would I know?" For several minutes I got caught up in the discussion of his directs when I became aware of two things—the first was how hard Carl was working—there were large dark circles under his armpits, and the second was "why on earth are his direct reports in a camper!" I hadn't asked Carl the most important question, "Why aren't your direct reports driving in the car with you?" He considered the question and the light dawned—he needed his team in the car with him; this would make him a better driver. "They could sit in the back," he said. I decided to push him further. "Would you," I asked, "let one of your directs drive the car while you sat in the passenger seat?" This was a configuration he had never considered and took us back full circle to his lack of self-awareness and how he was oblivious to the impact his behavior had on others in his business, as well as his direct reports. I've subsequently used the car analogy with other leaders I have worked with to illustrate not only the need to share the driving but to draw attention to how driving may impact others on the road.

The second question exists because we can only gauge our effect on others if they tell us about it, and we can only replicate a great performance when we understand what we did. For a number of years now I have worked with Chris and Cathy, two business analysts who used to work for the consulting firm McKenzie. They have never been clients, but I have learned a lot by observing how they work. After *every* presentation or meeting the two of them huddle together and give feedback on each other's performance—what they noticed, what went well, what they would change based upon their observations, and what should be the practical next step. Chris and Cathy are two of the most self-aware people I have met because they realize the importance of feedback for their own growth as well as continued business success. They also realize feedback cannot wait until midyear performance evaluations or end-of-year reviews; it has to become part of a person's daily routine to be truly effective. The third and final question probes clients' openness to feedback. Do they become defensive when they are given advice? Do they interpret feedback as criticism, something to avoid or get angry about? If they make a mistake is it always someone else's fault? Without the ability to really hear feedback a client will make little progress—with me or on the job.

HOW SELF-AWARE ARE YOU?

To help my clients develop greater a working knowledge of self-awareness I often use a model called The Johari Window.[2] The model is named after its two inventors, psychologists Joseph Luft and Harry Ingram, and conceptualizes self-awareness as four windowpanes, each pane representing a different type of awareness. These are:

1. *Open.* Things I know about myself (or think I know), which I freely share or disclose with others. These aren't just facts, for example my age, where I live, or my phone number, but also my interests or how I feel about certain issues.

2. *Blind.* Things others know about me of which I'm not aware. We can also refer to these as blind spots. These range from the trivial—a mark on the back of my jacket that I cannot see but you can—to the significant. I ask and answer all my own questions, causing people to feel disempowered and frustrated. Blind is possibly the most dangerous pane, as we are unaware of the impact we are having on others. This means in a key meeting with my manager I may be having exactly the impact I wanted, or I may be turning him against my plan because of the way I am communicating or behaving; I don't know. To avoid or reduce the size of this pane, it's important to continually ask for and be open to feedback, and monitor the impact we are having on people by "mindreading," a psychological skill we all have and which I say more about later in this chapter. Looking through the "blind" window means that we are doomed to repeat the same mistakes and stagnate personally and professionally. A rule of thumb is that if you are often surprised by people's comments about you then you have a fairly large blind spot.

3. *Hidden.* Things I know about myself but keep concealed from others. For example, if I've just met someone, I will likely not confide my most private personal thoughts and aspirations. As I get to know them better, I may eventually choose to share this information. Or maybe I never will. It may be that it never occurs to me that someone else might find this information interesting or relevant. How long we stay behind the "hidden" pane usually reveals how much or how little we are willing to trust others. We'll examine the issue of trust in chapter 5.

4. *Unknown.* Things neither I nor others know about me. Some information lies in the unconscious, and we become aware of it through dreams or therapy.

Figure 4.1 The Window Model

	Known to Self	Not known to Self
Known to others	Open	Blind
Not known to others	Hidden	Unknown

The model is summarized in Figure 4.1.

When a client is struggling with self-awareness issues I will quickly draw the model on a white board and ask them to tell me how open, hidden, or blind they feel they are. For example, Josh believed that work and his personal life should be kept separate. He was a fairly shy person who didn't enjoy socializing with the team or talking about himself. The problem was that his team had no way to get to know Josh, which made it hard for them to attach to their leader, to trust him, or be able to understand more about his motivations, passion and aspirations. Using the window model, I explained to Josh that he had a very small Open pane, a large Hidden pane, and a fairly large Blind pane, because he didn't understand how his fierce sense of privacy was hurting his relationship with the team. Ultimately, we increased the size of the Open windowpane and reduced the size of the Blind and Hidden quadrants, primarily by getting him comfortable with expressing his beliefs to his team so they could understand him better.

Now, it's important to understand that changing this open/hidden/blind dynamic isn't about "opening the kimono" to the point of inappropriate self-disclosure. It's about sharing your life experience so that people understand you better. Some people feel compelled to share everything about themselves, believing it enables them to connect deeply with others. Sharing at a level out of all proportion to the needs of the relationship can result in inappropriate self-disclosure, what some people jokingly refer to as TMI—Too Much Information. The result is that your need for openness forces other people to keep themselves "hidden" in order to protect themselves.

BEHAVIORAL SIGNATURES

Managers often complain to me that they're sure they could avoid all kinds of unexpected surprises and manage relationships better if they could just learn how to read other people. My reply is that they already know how to read people, they're just not paying attention to what they see.

A self-aware leader has to be a bit of a detective. Through our voice, our body language, and our facial expressions, every one of us leaves clues that announce to the world how we feel and what we are thinking at any given moment. These clues are collectively referred to as behavioral signatures.[3] The three most important clues a self-aware leader should become cognizant of are interpersonal style, boundaries, and attachment behavior. By following these clues, a self-aware leader can learn everything she needs to know about her team and what they need from her.

Interpersonal Style

Our interpersonal style determines how people perceive us, how they relate and respond to us, whether they listen or ignore us—in short, whether they pay attention to and are influenced by us and what we do and say. While there are an almost infinite number of subtleties and nuances associated with a person's interpersonal style, I have generalized them into three categories—passive, assertive, and aggressive. Each style is a combination of behavior and the beliefs we hold about ourselves and other people, and each style says something about us and our perceptions of others with whom we work.

The Passive Style

A person with a passive style[4] usually finds it impossible to take a stand or challenge others, or makes proposals in such a way that others easily disregard or ignore them. They might express their ideas in an apologetic, diffident, or self-effacing way. People who are passive often use self-canceling messages, contradictory or invalidating statements tacked on to a proposal, idea or suggestion, such as "I don't really know anything about this but here's what I think" or "We could shift the focus of our strategy, but that's just my opinion." Passive communication makes it very easy for other people to discard your ideas because you have already done it for them.

Passive people's beliefs about others include:

- The ideas, needs, and requests of others are more important than their own.
- Others have rights but they do not.
- They have little or nothing to contribute to a decision or proposal; other people have a great deal to contribute.
- Without external approval, they have no worth.

People who rely on a passive interpersonal style are anxious to avoid conflict and please others. Receiving praise and validation, especially from our significant others—a partner, friend, work colleague, or boss—is vital. The problem is that people with passive interpersonal styles often develop a chronic need to please, what I call the approval addiction. Such a dependency can make these individuals extremely vulnerable in their relationships. They often become compulsive care-givers or start overfunctioning. They engage in avoidance strategies, for example, repeatedly canceling meetings in which they know they have to relay an unpopular message. Sometimes they'll try to hide their dependency by becoming aggressive. Other people shut down emotionally in order to protect themselves from feelings of disapproval.

The Assertive Style

An assertive style represents the sweet spot on a continuum between passive and aggressive behavior. People often equate assertion with behavior that provokes conflict or tension; in fact, it's quite the opposite. For example, giving someone positive feedback is assertive. So is giving or receiving compliments. Other assertive behavior might be admitting personal shortcomings, initiating and maintaining relationships, expressing positive emotions, being unafraid to communicate unpopular messages, requesting behavior changes in others you work with, and refusing unreasonable requests.[5]

An assertive leader's beliefs about others include

- The ideas, needs, and requests of other people are important, but no more important than their own;
- other people's ideas and ways of doing things are just as valid as their own; and
- they have something to contribute to the running of the business, and so do the people they work with.

People with an assertive style know how to challenge another person's thinking in a respectful way. They are comfortable disagreeing or saying no to an idea or request. They are comfortable giving and receiving honest feedback, and they don't worry about being unpopular. They are excellent problem solvers, and understand how to avoid personal attacks when arguing with someone else.

Assertive people maintain a healthy, respectful relationship with others—but not at all costs. Many people confuse assertion with aggression, but they are not the same thing. An aggressive person is driven by the intense desire to win, to come out on top by any means possible. This often means belittling or diminishing coworkers. Assertive leaders are far more objective and rational, seeking the win-win but also making sure other people know they are not pushovers.

The Aggressive Style

People who communicate with an aggressive style usually ignore the needs, wants, opinions, feelings, or beliefs of others in favor of their own. They express their needs and desires in inappropriate ways. For example, they'll put people down, or be deliberately hurtful or critical if it gets them what they want. They also often blame others for their own shortcomings. Above all, they want to control and retain power over other people.

Their beliefs about themselves and others include:

- Their needs, wants, and opinions are more important than anybody else's.
- They have rights but others do not.
- They have something to contribute; other people have little or nothing to contribute.

Closely related to aggressive interpersonal style is passive-aggressiveness. Passive-aggressive people have a hard time expressing

126

their anger, frustration, or discomfort, so their emotions tend to leak out in indirect, destructive ways. Classic passive-aggressive behaviors include selective memory, in which we remember what we want to remember and forget what we want to forget; habitual unapologetic tardiness; and backhanded compliments or hostile remarks followed by "I'm just kidding," or "Can't you take a joke?"

CHOOSING YOUR INTERPERSONAL STYLE

In my experience problems with assertion are twofold. Some clients have a predisposition to lack assertion across all situations. In these cases the problem stems from a personality trait or characteristic. The second and more frequent problem occurs when a client is unaware that his behavior clashes or is inappropriate to the needs of the situation. For example, he is passive when his team needs him to be decisive or forceful, or aggressive when he needs to be more deferential. Here's a good rule of thumb: The more uncomfortable you are with what someone asks of you, such as staying late at the office on your spouse's birthday, the more assertive you need to be.

To help clients become more aware of whether they are passive, assertive, or aggressive I draw the following scale on a piece of paper or white board:

Passive	Assertive	Aggressive
0	10	20

Then I ask them to use the scale to rate their interpersonal style. For example, if they usually avoid saying no, aim to please, or are anxious to be approved of, they might rate themselves somewhere between 0 and 5; if they are often able to say no, or able to stick up for their rights, then their rating might fall between 10 and 13. A more aggressive person, one who talks over others, and/or harangues or criticizes to get her own way, might rank anywhere from 16 to 20. After clients have rated themselves, I then ask them to consider where they wish they were on the scale. How assertive must they be to be effective at their job? Occasionally they reply with the same rating, but usually there is a gap. We then discuss what action they can take to increase or decrease their assertiveness. We try to find out if their aggressiveness or passivity flares up with certain people; we explore how they might make themselves more vulnerable to their teams. I'll often assign homework, asking the client to keep track of where she rates throughout the week as she comes into contact with different people and situations. In this way, we can reduce their blind spots.

Aishwarga's case is a good example of how this method works in practice. I was observing her in a meeting with one of her directs and at the end of the conversation I asked if I could pose a couple of questions. The first was a standard question. Did this represent a typical meeting or had my presence altered the dynamic between them in any way? They replied that their meeting had been typical. The second was a more pointed question to Aishwarga's direct, Peru. Did he have any feedback for Aishwarga that would improve their meetings? Initially he was slow to respond, but after a short time he replied that Aishwarga's mind seemed to drift elsewhere during their meetings. I, too, had observed how hard it was for her to ignore the constant stream of e-mail that popped up on her monitor. Then Peru added that he particularly noticed this habit when he dropped by her office for a chat. It was at this moment that I guessed that Aishwarga's problem might be with her level of assertion. I asked Peru, "How would you feel if Aishwarga said to you. 'Peru, I can't talk now, I have to finish these e-mails. Let's meet in an hour when we can sit down and I can give you my full attention.' " "I wouldn't be happy," he replied. "I'd think I had done something wrong. I'd be upset."

It was clear to me that Aishwarga and Peru were involved in a struggle. Peru needed Aishwarga's time and attention and Aishwarga didn't know how to refuse. She was enabling Peru's neediness with her passivity. Unfortunately, by dividing her attention she could focus neither on her e-mail nor on Peru. Peru wasn't my client—there wasn't much I could do to curb his passive-aggressiveness. But I could help Aishwarga improve her assertiveness. We looked at the "Passive—Assertive—Aggressive" scale together. She rated herself as a 5, but felt she would be more effective as a 10. We practiced a number of responses she could give to Peru and others when they dropped in unannounced, and worked on steeling her emotionally so she didn't feel so guilty when she refused or deferred a request. The other thing I suggested was that she shut her door. Like a lot of companies, Microsoft has an open door policy, a practice which became popular in the mid-1980s, in an attempt to speed up communication, heighten morale, and promote idea sharing. But the open door, so key to spontaneous brainstorming, is also an invitation for disruption. In addition, nowadays anyone who does choose to close their door risks being labeled as uncooperative, distant, or inaccessible. It takes a great deal of assertiveness to fight such an ingrained cultural norm. By closing her door, though, Aishwarga was able to train everyone to respect her time by clearly delineating when she would be available for drop-in visits, and when she needed to remain undisturbed.

BOUNDARIES: THE SPACE BETWEEN

Aishwarga's story also illustrates how our styles are related to the way we manage our boundaries. A boundary, of course, is often used to describe a dividing line between objects. A boundary may also describe a dividing line between one person and another—a metaphorical wall or fence.[6] Social boundaries foster the growth and maintenance of good relationships and protect us from bad ones.[7] Without boundaries we obstruct the development of healthy, reciprocal relationships.

TYPES OF BOUNDARY

Salvador Minuchin, the family therapist who has had such an impact on STCT, proposed that boundaries exist on a continuum.[8] At one extreme are "enmeshed" boundaries, where autonomy is sacrificed for closeness. At the other extreme are "disengaged" boundaries, where individuals are emotionally and physically distant from one another. Between the two extremes are "clear" boundaries where individuals can balance their need for autonomy with healthy relationships. Disengaged boundaries are characterized by chronic individuality. People with these types of boundaries are likely to have little attachment or commitment to others, and have little expectation that others can be counted on for affirmation or support. Conversely, enmeshed or diffuse boundaries lead to overdependency and overinvolvement. For example, Aishwarga was unable to separate her feelings from those of Peru. She felt guilty that she might upset him by saying no. By adopting a passive interpersonal style and choosing an enmeshed boundary Aishwarga revealed that she prioritized closeness above autonomy, was willing to sacrifice effectiveness and influence for approval, and would put the needs of her direct reports above her own. This aspect of her personality had remained in the "hidden" pane of the four quadrants that made up her self-awareness until I made her think about it.

So how can leaders become more aware of their boundaries when they don't have someone like me pointing out the implications of their actions and choices?

Managing Your Boundaries

There is generally an unspoken agreement about how much physical space there should be between you and the people you meet in your day-to-day life. We don't continue walking toward each other until our faces are about an inch apart before beginning our conversation. Yet we've all complained about someone invading our personal space, which is just another way of saying that someone has just trampled all over our boundaries. The physical space or boundary we have between ourselves and the other people in our lives varies depending on our relationship with that person. It is more likely that we would allow a thinner boundary between us and our partner than with a complete stranger. The more comfortable or intimate the relationship, the easier it is for us to bear closeness.

It's relatively easy for leaders to determine what type of boundary they prefer. If they

- want to be friends with their subordinates or direct reports rather than manage the hierarchy and act like a leader;
- worry about personal relationships when making tough decisions;

- avoid conflict in favor of approval;
- want to be included in every decision;
- prize loyalty and consensus above independent thought and action;
- believe there is no "I" in team; and
- disclose details about themselves that may be inappropriate

then they have a preference for more enmeshed boundaries. If they

- have little interest in getting to know people they work with or vice versa;
- prefer to keep to themselves, drawing a strong dividing line between work and their personal life;
- have few expectations that people will deliver and live by the maxim "If you want something done do it yourself"; and
- see little benefit in teamwork

then they have a preference for more disengaged boundaries. If they

- recognize when the people they work with need help or support without becoming overinvolved and solving their problem;
- are open with subordinates or direct reports about their beliefs and can illustrate what matters to them through stories drawn from their life experience;
- are comfortable talking about their life outside of work but know the difference between appropriate and inappropriate disclosure;
- can make the tough calls but recognize that their decisions impact people; and
- realize that they can't be successful on their own, acknowledging that to succeed they must empower the people who work for them and accept different styles of execution

then they have clear boundaries.

A classic article by William Oncken, Jr. and Donald L. Wass for the *Harvard Business Review*, intended as a cautionary tale of how managers lose time by adopting the burdens, or "monkeys," of their subordinates, is also a wonderful depiction of poor boundary management.[9] It begins with the following scenario:

> A manager is on his way to a meeting when he bumps into one of his directs, Jones. After exchanging brief pleasantries Jones comments, "By the way, we've got a problem." He goes on to describe the issue and ask for help. Eventually, the manager says, "So glad you brought this up. I'm in a rush right now. Meanwhile, let me think about it, and I'll let you know."

Prior to the meeting the monkey was firmly on Jones' back, but after the exchange the monkey belongs to the manager. The transfer was possible because of the poorly defined boundaries between the two. It all starts in a fairly innocuous fashion with Jones explaining, "We've got a problem." However, this opening comment marks the start of the monkey being passed from subordinate to manager. In reality the manager didn't have a problem; Jones did. But the use of "we" indicates Jones sees this as a shared problem with joint accountability. If at this point the manager had replied, "What problem do you have?" or suggested that they meet later, he would have been acting assertively, drawing a clear boundary between himself and Jones and between the monkey and its proper owner. Instead, because of a case of enmeshed boundaries, the manager has now taken responsibility for Jones' monkey.

ATTACHMENT RELATIONSHIPS

The third and final component of a person's behavioral signature is his attachment style—the degree to which a person can develop close, trusting relationships with others. British psychoanalyst John Bowlby developed attachment theory in the 1960s and 1970s.[10] Bowlby challenged the thinking in child psychiatry at that time, which characterized the distress infants expressed when separated from their parents as an immature coping strategy. He proposed instead that a baby's cries were a purposeful attempt to reestablish connection or proximity to the missing parent. Bowlby went on to develop a comprehensive model that explained individual differences in attachment style. For example, overprotective, cold, and inconsistent parents will create a sense of insecure attachment in their infants. These children often grow to be anxious and clingy, preferring to stay close to their parents rather than explore the world around them. Conversely, nurturing, supportive parents who provide what Bowlby calls a "secure base"— like a base camp where explorers can return following their journey or if inclement weather threatens—allow the child freedom to explore, which helps them become independent, sociable, and confident. Bowlby termed this type of behavior secure attachment. Over time Bowlby identified three types of attachment style—secure, anxious-ambivalent, and avoidant. The secure child is playful, uninhibited, and sociable; the anxious-ambivalent infant is less secure, easily distracted and fears rejection; and the avoidant child is less compliant, more independent, and less likely to seek out comfort or contact with her parents.

So why is attachment so important to understanding our behavioral signature? Because childhood patterns of attachment are significant predictors of later adult attachment style.[11] Consequently there is a significant likelihood that the anxious or insecure child will grow up to be an anxious or insecure adult. The characteristics of adult attachment behaviors are as follows:

- Adults with a secure attachment have few self-doubts and high self-esteem. They are usually liked by others, can develop trusting, intimate relationships, and are able to balance closeness with independence.

- Anxious-ambivalent adults are passive, motivated by a desire for approval, and they fear rejection. They tend to have poor insight, often seeing other people as complex and difficult to understand.

- Avoidant individuals tend to shy away from social situations because they lack confidence in their social skills. They tend to doubt the honesty and integrity of other people and rely almost exclusively on their own judgment. People with an avoidant attachment style compensate for their fears of rejection by emphasizing their achievements.

To date most of the studies into adult attachment behavior have focused on romantic relationships and problems with intimacy. There is one study, however, that has monitored the implications of adult attachment style for performance in the workplace, and which has proven valuable in my work.[12] The study found that of the three groups studied, securely attached respondents had a more positive approach to work than groups exhibiting other attachment styles. These individuals were least likely to put off work, least likely to have difficulty completing tasks, and least likely to fear rejection from colleagues or worry about failure. They enjoyed vacations and did not allow work to jeopardize their relationships or health. The anxious-ambivalent sample worried about their work performance, felt underappreciated, were easily distracted and tended to slack off after receiving positive feedback. The avoidant subjects preferred to work alone and used work as an excuse to avoid having friends or a social life.

To determine a client's attachment preference I examine the results from their 360 surveys along with the results of a brief questionnaire in which I ask my clients to read through each of the following statements and identify which one most closely resembles the way they prefer to conduct their relationships at work.[13]

- *Statement 1*: I find it relatively easy to get close to others at work and am comfortable depending on them and having them depend on me. I don't often worry about being isolated or about someone getting too close to me.

- *Statement 2*: I am fairly uncomfortable being close to others at work and am nervous or uncomfortable when anyone wants to get too close, or people want to be friendlier than I like. In general I prefer to be left to my own devices. I find it difficult to trust the others I work with and generally doubt the honesty and integrity of coworkers. Achievement is far more important then the quality of work relationships.

- *Statement 3*: I find that others are reluctant to get as close to me as I would like. I often worry that people I work with don't really like me, or won't want to work with me. I want more from my work relationships than other people are prepared to give, and this sometimes makes people uncomfortable.

People who check statement #1 are likely to have secure relationships with people. This means that they are likely to approach relationships from a position of trust and considerable self-confidence.

Statement #2 reflects a more avoidant pattern. People who check it prioritize work above all else. They like to be kept busy and are made uncomfortable when they are asked to work with others or be part of a team. Statement #3 indicates a more anxious or ambivalent attitude to relationships. Those who identify with this statement are overly focused on the praise and judgments of others, which often leaves them feeling underappreciated. Preoccupation with relationships can be distracting and prevent them from finishing work on time. They have a strong preference for working with others or being part of a team.

BECOMING SELF-AWARE

Becoming self-aware—understanding and acknowledging our interpersonal style, boundaries, and attachment behavior—is essential if we want to reduce the size of our blind spot, have an impact on our coworkers and colleagues, and understand the implications of our behavioral signature. Without knowing whether we are passive or assertive, enmeshed or securely attached, we have little way of understanding why we do what we do, nor are we able to predict with any degree of certainty how other people will respond to our behavior. We certainly can't be adaptable. Paradoxically, self-aware people are not only cognizant of their ownselves, but also cognizant of others, and prepared to change or modify their behavior style according to the needs of any situation. By fully understanding ourselves—our motivations, beliefs and history, our relationship with success, our blind spots—we become less self-absorbed. We don't feel the need to focus all our attention internally on our needs, our feelings, and our personal agenda. This awareness means we have the opportunity to pay attention to the people we work with.

READING OTHERS, READING YOURSELF

Over the past ten years Dr. Jo-Ellan Dimitrius has been in court for attempted murder, rape, larceny, and brutality. In every occasion she has used her skills to influence the jury. Dimitrius is widely regarded as one of the top trial consultants in North America. Her job is to read people and, in the five minutes available to her in the pretrial phase, determine whether a juror would give her client a fair hearing. "A wrong decision," she says, "could literally be fatal to my client." In her book *Reading People*, she explains:

> Some of those who read people for a living, as I do, rely almost exclusively on scientific research, surveys, studies, polls, and statistical analysis. Others claim to have a God-given talent. My own experience has taught me that reading people is neither a science nor an innate gift. It is a matter of knowing what to look and listen for, having the curiosity and patience to gather the necessary information, and understanding how to recognize the patterns in a person's appearance, body language, voice, and conduct.[14]

The ability to understand and predict the behavior of other people is of crucial importance in business. Leaders are constantly evaluating others. Who to hire? Who to promote? Who to trust? I am often asked to help improve clients' ability to read other people. One of my favorite exercises in team therapy is to ask people to partner up, preferably with someone they don't know, or someone they feel is very different from them. They are then instructed to sit facing one another and to decide who will go first. Basing their guess solely on the physical clues they see in front of them, Person A then has two minutes to describe Person B—what kind of books this person may read, his favorite movie, what his ambition was growing up. Person B is not to reveal whether Person A is right or wrong. After two minutes, the partners swap roles. After Person B has finished, they each reveal the accuracy of the other's assessment. When we debrief the exercise we generally find that several things have happened:

- We often transfer our likes and dislikes onto others. For example, because I like mystery novels I assume you do, too. These projections tell us everything about ourselves and nothing about the person we are talking to, as I never ask you to tell me what you like.
- Self-aware individuals tend to more accurately assess other people, as they are less self-absorbed and therefore able to pick up the subtleties of other people's behavior.
- People look for similarities and forget or overlook differences.
- In general, people are good at reading others.

So the question is, if most of us can mindread during the course of this exercise, why do we find it so difficult to read others on a day-to-day basis in the workplace? For most of us, it is because we are self-absorbed. This doesn't mean that people are inherently selfish or uncaring, but rather they are too focused on the task at hand—getting through the report, finishing the meeting, closing down questions—to be really aware of the world outside. I've sat in many meetings where managers drone on despite the fact that the participants are shifting in their seats, looking at their watches, doodling on note pads, or playing solitaire on their laptops. It's obvious that they (and I) would rather be anywhere else. And yet, because of his lack of awareness, the manager goes on without changing course.

Deepak wanted to improve his ability to read others. He was good at adapting his interpersonal style to the requirements of the different meetings he attended but found it very difficult to shift gears *during* a meeting. He wanted to become what I call a "switcher," someone who is so aware of the reaction of others to his words or actions that he can effortlessly change his approach in midstream. To be able to "switch awareness" from yourself to others, you have to have confidence, you have to know what makes you tick, and above all, you have to remember to check at regular intervals to see how people are responding to you.

MINDBLINDNESS AND THEORY OF MIND

In his book entitled *Mindblindness*, psychiatrist Simon Baron-Cohen asks us to "imagine what [our] world would be like if [we] were aware of physical things but were blind to the existence of mental things like the thoughts, beliefs, knowledge, desires and intentions [of others]."[15] In other words, what would it be like if we could describe in detail the brushstrokes on a painting or the grain on a piece of wood, but couldn't understand why anyone would want to hug us? This is how life is experienced by people with autism, a disease which impacts a child's or adult's ability to socialize, communicate, and infer the thoughts and motives of others. Baron-Cohen's work has also helped psychologists understand how people who do not suffer from this disease make sense of their social world. Psychologists call the ability to recognize and make sense of the beliefs, thoughts, and feelings of others the Theory of Mind (TOM) or "mindreading." This ability is directly related to attachment style—securely attached individuals are better able to read the behavior and facial expressions of others. I use the terms mindblind and mindreading with my clients to help them understand that though we are all born psychologists, with the ability to read others' moods and feelings from a very early age, our behavior and emotions often short-circuit this innate ability in adulthood. Low self-confidence, "Hurry-Sickness" (characterized by an almost manic need to multitask and move as quickly as possible from one activity to another), our interpersonal style, or twisted thoughts cause us to ignore the huge amount of information we are constantly processing about the social world around us—information that, if we paid attention, could help us adapt our communication style or behavior to more closely match the needs of other people.

As I explained to Deepak, though, we can relearn how to use our mindreading skills by following just a few simple rules. But it can be overwhelming at first to know just what to focus on. For example, the human face can make 43 distinct muscle movements that can be combined into more than 10,000 facial configurations.[16]

WHAT'S IN A FACE?

As I do with all of my clients who want to improve their ability to read others I asked Deepak to keep a record of what he noticed in his meetings. Whenever he was in a meeting, every five to ten minutes he was to consciously shift his awareness from what he was thinking and feeling, to what he noticed others might be thinking or feeling. To do this I recommended he focus on people's communication styles, specific behaviors, and most importantly, their faces. People's facial expressions are a particularly rich source of information about how they are feeling. (Charles Darwin was the first scientist to recognize that the expressions of happiness, surprise, anger, sadness, fear, and disgust were the same across the world.[17]) It's also interesting to note that studies of deception and lying have found that most people do not censor their body movements. So all in all we have a rich seam of uncensored information from which to mindread. To help Deepak decode the expressions and behaviors of his colleagues I asked him to do the following:

- When trying to infer someone's emotional state, use statements beginning with "He seems," "She looks," and "He sounds."
- How are people communicating? Are they hesitant, quiet, or loud? Do they speak quickly or slowly? Who isn't talking? What aspect of what you are talking about do they seem to find most interesting?
- What is the mood in the room? How do people seem? If the mood seems tense examine why that might be. Is someone dominating the conversation? Is the outcome of the meeting unclear? Is your mood infecting the group? Are people not listening to one another?

Many clients initially find it very hard to run a meeting and mindread at the same time, but over time they become more adept at it. To help Deepak learn to match his behavioral signature to the needs of the moment we went over his notes and I had him listen to a self-instructional training CD developed by Paul Ekman,[18] which is designed to improve the ability to recognize facial expressions.[19] We also watched one of my favorite movies, *Twelve Angry Men*. The movie, in which twelve jurors are sequestered in a room without air conditioning on a hot summer day to decide whether a defendant is guilty or innocent, is a particularly useful teaching aid as there is an abundance of different facial expressions, emotion, communication styles, and behavioral signatures on display.

FURTHER IMPLICATIONS OF OUR BEHAVIORAL SIGNATURE

This chapter has illustrated four of the five returns on investment (ROI) of self-awareness, as established by Chris Connelly and John Syer[20]:

1. An understanding of the self;
2. an appreciation of the self;
3. an understanding of others; and
4. an appreciation of the differences between us.

Without a robust sense of self and a clear understanding of our behavioral signature we cannot shift our attention away from our own wants, needs, and fears. Conversely, when we are securely attached, when we have clear boundaries and an assertive interpersonal style, we can be aware of the intentions, needs, responses, and emotions of others, an awareness that is crucial to great leadership because it allows for adaptability. It also reduces our blind spot so that we have a 360-degree view of where we're going, and whether anyone else is following.

The fifth ROI, trust, is the subject of the following chapter.

SELF-AWARENESS: THINGS TO THINK ABOUT

Self-aware leaders focus less on themselves than on the people they lead. They are acutely aware of the impact they have on others they work with and can change their behavior depending on the needs of a particular person or situation.

1. How often do you think about how your behavior affects every-one around you? Would you say that people generally do what you expect, or do you find you're often surprised by their actions?

2. Using the Johari window model, which pane would you say is the largest for you? Which is the smallest? Do you tend to keep much of yourself hidden? How might you disclose more about who you are and what you stand for?

3. Using the rating scale on page 127 how would you describe your interpersonal style? Are you generally passive, assertive, or aggressive in your relationships with others? Where do you think you would be more effective? What might you have to do differently to bridge this gap? Are there particular people who impact your style, both positively and negatively?

4. Shadow yourself throughout the day, using the exercise described on page 29, and watch for times when you are able to adapt your interpersonal style at a moment's notice. What made it easy for you to shift your approach?

5. How often do you make yourself available for feedback about your performance at work? How did you respond the last time you were criticized—did you close down, defend yourself, or find some truth in what was being said?

6. How would you rate the frequency of feedback in your business or team? If it is infrequent, how might you increase the occurrence of feedback?

7. How would you describe the attachment relationship you have with your team or subordinates? Review the statements on page 136 and select the one that best applies to you. Do you think this type of attachment relationship brings the best out in people? If not, what do you need to change? How would you describe the quality of attachment

in your organization? Are people generally secure or are they anxious? Are there areas of the business where people might be more vulnerable to insecure attachment?

8. Think about a problem you are wrestling with right now. How did the problem make its way onto your desk? Is it really your problem or did you allow someone to hand it to you? If so, can you pinpoint the moment it happened? What could you have done or said differently? What could you do now to transfer the responsibility for this problem to the right person?

9. How much does the approval of others motivate your behavior? What about your direct reports or subordinates—how much does it motivate theirs?

5

Trust

The Glue That Holds Us Together

Maximizing our authority and commanding respect relies heavily on being able to draw from our understanding of the first three universal issues that characterize great leadership that we've covered in this book—strong, well-articulated beliefs, high levels of confidence, and high levels of self-awareness. Ultimately, they all lay the groundwork for the fourth characteristic, Trust—the trust we have for others, and the trust others have in us. Communicating a set of clearly-held beliefs helps people trust that they know we stand for and what they can hope to achieve under our leadership. Confidence promotes within us and others a sense of security, which enables trusting relationships to grow and flourish. Self-awareness allows people to trust that we mean what we say and will do, what we promise to do ensuring relationships remain healthy.

In his book *Trust*, Francis Fukuyama, an American political philosopher, economist, and author, describes trust as the glue of any properly functioning society.[1] Yet levels of trust appear to be dropping precipitously. Harvard University found that 58 percent of the American public don't trust their leaders,[2] perceiving them as corrupt, out of touch with the needs of the public, and motivated by greed. When asked what they wanted most from their leaders, the public responded, "Honesty and integrity." They reported that they have the most trust in military and medical leaders, and the least trust in media and business leaders. These statistics are not specific to the United States. A global opinion survey revealed that the public's trust in global corporations has dropped sharply in Spain, Canada, Brazil, Germany, and the United Kingdom, while remaining strongest in China and India.[3]

So what do these data have to do with the clients I see in my practice? Trust may be the glue of any properly functioning society, but it is also the glue of any properly functioning organization, business, or team, and it's important to recognize the implications of trust and mistrust for micro- as well as macroeconomics. The significance of trust for organizational health is critical. When people trust each other and their leaders they can work through disagreements faster, take smarter risks, work harder, have greater loyalty, and contribute better ideas.[4] They are securely attached. The costs of mistrust are equally significant. Cynicism, turf protection, infighting, and an overly burdensome bureaucracy lead to insecure attachments and waste huge amounts of time, resources, and good will.

I've never had a client come to me and say, "I'm not trustworthy, can you help me?" We all think we can be trusted. Rather, problems related to trust hide in plain sight, the results of poorly managed expectations, poorly implemented or inconsistent leadership, and baggage from our past colliding with relationships in the present. In

148

this chapter I describe how failure to overcome these three problems impacts the climate of trust between people and within teams, then follow up with a look at the typical enemies of trust. But first, let's clarify what I mean when I speak about trust.

WHAT IS TRUST?

Trust is often easier to experience than to describe. Even psychologists have a hard time agreeing on what the term actually means.[5] Trust has been defined as an attitude; a behavior synonymous with confidence; and as a set of beliefs. I describe it as a spoken or unspoken contract between people that permits them to articulate their expectations. It means they feel safe confiding in, being vulnerable with, giving feedback to, or disagreeing with each other. But as my therapist often told me, "There is no trust without doubt." At the time his remark seemed like a contradiction. If I trust you why would I doubt your veracity? If I doubt you, then why would I confide in you? It took me a few years to figure out what he was getting at—that to trust *is* to risk. My clients trust that I will be competent, that I will listen without judgment, that I am well intentioned and unlikely to harm them. Yet they can't predict with certainty what the outcome of our relationship might be. They have faith that I will safeguard their confidences and not report back to their manager or colleagues about the problems with which they are struggling. The same is true of any workplace relationship. There is no trust without some risk that a colleague might use our self-disclosure to gain advantage or power over us. Yet how comfortable we are taking risks is only one part of what impacts our levels of trust.

In their article "The Enemies of Trust," Rob Galford and Anne Drapeau suggest that leaders need to protect trustworthiness "because trust takes years to build but can suffer serious damage in a moment."[6] I don't believe trust has to take years to build—most leaders and managers don't have the luxury of years to develop trusting relationships with their subordinates; most have a matter of months. Moreover, it seems from my experience many people find it relatively easy to trust. I had a client describe this belief as his "trust bank." He explained that his coworkers all started out with healthy "bank balances," but if their behavior caused him to lose trust then they made a withdrawal on their trust account. Over time the balance could remain in the black or go into the red if trust was completely drained. That's another facet of trust—it's dynamic. Just because I trust you today doesn't mean I will have the same amount of faith or belief in you tomorrow; yet it is also important to recognize that the trust bank doesn't go into the red immediately. The size of the withdrawal depends on your behavior—a misstep followed by an apology may mean a small withdrawal whereas a significant breach of confidence will mean you go in the red and stay there.

We also have to consider the organizational context itself. Unlike friendships or relationships that occur outside of work, people at work must decide whether to rely on others of whom they know little and with whom they have little personal history.[7] Even managers at the highest levels don't always get to choose who they work with. Globalization has made this problem even more acute as corporate networks have become more widespread and relationships have become more virtual. As Charles Handy, a fellow of the London Business School, asks, "How do you manage people who you cannot see?" He answers his own question. "By trusting them."[8] If I've learned anything from my work around the world it's that most people are willing to go out of their way to make up for the uncertainties caused by virtual relationships, mostly by taking a plane, train, or automobile trip. We may live in a digital age, but bosses at the biggest corporate giants travel up to five days a week in order to meet their business partners face to face.[9] Many managers "forsake the convenience of e-mail for the discomfort of air travel because they presume nothing succeeds in creating trust better than eyeball-to-eyeball contact."[10] When I work with teams whose membership spans the globe, by far the biggest goal is to give participants a chance to get to know one another, to put a face to the name. It's far easier to trust a person than an e-mail alias. One of my favorite exercises is called A Day In The Life, where each team member is given a disposable camera and asked to take pictures that capture what a "normal" day looks like in Japan, India, Brazil, Germany, or France, including outside of work. Sharing these storyboards helps build relationships, familiarity, and trust. A high-trust organization evolves from a balance between high tech and high touch.

In the end, trust takes commitment, consistency, and, on occasion, no small amount of courage. Consider for a moment who you trust at work. Why do you trust them? Are there people you don't trust? I introduced an exericse in chapter 1 that goes to the heart of trust relationships in a team or business. It's called Team Geometry. I ask my client to draw a circle on a whiteboard or piece of paper and put herself at the center of the circle. I then invite her to put everyone who reports to her in the circle, positioning them according to how much or how little trust exists within the relationship. The closer they are to my client in the center the more trusting the relationship; the further away, the less the client trusts or feels trusted by them. I also use this technique in real time, with members of the team present, to map out the quality and direction of trust. This is one of my favorite exercises, one that outs, in an extremely visible way, problematic trust relationships. From here we know exactly where to begin.

There are three ways a leader can establish or reestablish trust:

- Manage Expectations;
- acknowledge and accept differences; and
- let go of the past.

Manage Expectations

Many leaders come to me for help in building high-performance teams, which are characterized by close, trusting relationships. There are three stages to the process. The first is Direction Setting, which clarifies a leader's vision, purpose, and beliefs for the rest of the team. The second stage is Relationship Building, which focuses on developing trust between team members. The final stage is Reaching Out, which concentrates on developing strong trust relationships with other teams, businesses, or partners. Relationship Building is most germane to our discussion of trust. The cornerstone of this step is identifying and then managing expectations, both yours and those of the people you lead. We earn each other's trust by communicating expectations clearly and then consistently meeting those expectations. Unfortunately, all too often our expectations—what we need from one another—remain unspoken, and unspoken expectations are impossible to fulfill. I've met a number of leaders who complain that their subordinates are not delivering. In subsequent meetings with their directs I find out they had never been explicitly told what they were expected to deliver. People often assume certain expectations based on a person's job title. Your subordinate might expect you to provide air cover if he is unfairly criticized by a colleague. Your expectation is that he is senior enough in the organization to look after himself.

Managing expectations is a two-way street. A leader needs people on his team to clearly articulate what they need from him. Similarly the leader needs to identify and communicate what he needs from his direct reports. There are two ways to gather this information. When I'm working with a newly formed team or a team struggling with low levels of trust, I first collect answers to the following questions using a web-based survey methodology:

- What do you need from your manager *to be successful* right now?
- Using a scale of zero to ten, how well is your manager delivering on this need?
- What do you believe you manager needs from you?

For a mature team in which relationships are more established I ask these questions live during a workshop or meeting. Every person writes down on a piece of paper what they need from their manager, and, using the rating scale of zero to ten, whether they are getting it; then one at a time they read out what they have written down. The manager's job is to listen, ask questions, and then give feedback. An important principle I emphasize in this process is that just because someone expresses a need doesn't immediately make it the manager's responsibility to fulfill that need. The main point of the exercise is to make everyone's expectations explicit. That's how a leader builds trust between himself and his team. A secondary goal is to build trust between team members. My experience with Guillaume and his team is a terrific example of how this process can clear up chronic misperceptions of expectations.

Guillaume was a physiological anomaly. He could go several days without sleeping and had a staggering capacity for work. It was not unusual to receive an e-mail from him sent at 1:00, 2:00, or 3:00 in the morning. Guillaume's problem wasn't his workload; it was the effect his workload was having on his team. He had good self-awareness. He knew he was overfunctioning—doing things for his team they could and should have been doing for themselves. He was also aware that members of the team worried about keeping up or felt that they had to be up at all hours to answer his e-mails. This was affecting the morale and trust within the team.

I sent each member a link to the survey questions. Table 5.1 summarizes their responses. Clearly, there were some areas where Guillaume excelled—listening to feedback, clarity of vision, and passion. Establishing trust, managing expectations and making himself accessible were not his strong suits.

Table 5.1 Survey Results

What the team needs from Guillaume to be successful	Are they getting it?
Constructive feedback	10
Clarity on the vision and first line tenets of the organization as a whole	9
Gain support from outside groups	9
Passion and confidence in team's potential to make a difference	9
Consistency in message/direction	8
Support when asked to push past resistance	8
Time together to help define strategy and direction for my team	6
Consistency	5
Critique and feedback on what I'm doing	5
Trust and confidence	4
Reasonable expectations re: delivery time	4
Regular meetings	4
Recognition of contribution	3
Timely, dependable information that I can act on	3
Accessibility—both scheduled and unscheduled	2
Creating a team culture	2

Guillaume and I reviewed the feedback. Some expectations were pretty clear-cut, for example, "Gain support from outside groups." For others he felt he needed more information. I circulated the table to the team and they came to a meeting prepared to discuss their feedback and hear Guillaume's response. He asked his reports to clarify some of their needs, for example, how regularly they wanted to meet with him, and what "accessibility" and "consistency" meant to them. Accuracy is important. The more precise the expectation the more it fosters trust and the contract that binds the participants together. There were a few items he resisted. He felt everyone was responsible for creating team culture. Though he understood people's desire for "unscheduled accessibility," he couldn't accommodate them. As a senior vice president in the company his time was booked months in advance and he didn't want to set an unrealistic expectation that he would be available at the drop of the hat. We were about to start discussing what Guillaume's expectations for the team were when it occurred to me that much of what his team was asking for was in direct response to his prodigious capacity for work. I raised the issue and the team had a full and frank exchange about how his style was hurting their confidence, making them worry that they couldn't keep up and feel inefficient. It was a relief to them to learn that Guillaume had no expectations that they work as intensely as he did. He worked ridiculous hours during the week so he could relax guilt-free with his family on the weekend. As long as the work got done, he didn't care what hours the rest of his team kept. This information took a huge load of worry and fear off of his teammates, freeing them to move forward with more confidence and trust in their leader.

Guillaume then presented his needs for the team. They were:

- Be responsible and accountable leaders of your organizations; set the example.
- Help each other achieve results; develop trust and respect for each other.
- Assume your seat at the table—don't rely on me to invite you to participate.
- Build process and people; don't try to carry the day relying only on your own IQ.
- Don't make me manage things.
- Honesty. I am not smart enough to deal with trickery and spin.
- Excellence in everything you do; acknowledge and learn from mistakes.
- Trust me and support decisions I make.
- Integrate with other departments and businesses in Microsoft.
- Build strong teams, don't tolerate mediocrity, and act early to build muscle.

After completing such an honest and rigorous examination, the worst thing in the world would be to allow everyone to slide back into old patterns. The clear expectations need to be maintained, embedded into the life of the team. They need to become part and parcel of the team norms—the way they do things. The Development Blueprint that I introduced in chapter 1 is an indispensable tool to keep people honest. In my experience even the most committed team can forget the expectations they established when they get back to the hurly-burly of the day job. The team creates a 30-, 60- and 90-day plan around their expectations that can be reviewed at regular intervals. The blueprint provides an explicit outline that the team can refer to in subsequent meetings to check progress and monitor accountability.

Acknowledge and Accept Differences

Who would you find it easier to trust, someone like you with a similar working style, or someone completely different? Most people gravitate to those who share some fundamental similarities with them. Studies into successful marital relationships all agree that similarities are the basis of a healthy, long-term relationship.[11] Unfortunately, most leaders I've worked with don't have the luxury of choosing their subordinates—they've usually inherited their team. Even when they have a hand in who to hire, their decisions are based on one or two meetings, geared toward assessing job competence, not whether the person will provide a close, trusting relationship.

Leaders have to accept that people do things differently; not better or worse, just differently. As one leader came to recognize, "You must hire [or] develop strong managers [and] then allow them to have true empowerment. They may not always make the right decision or one that you'd make, but you have to allow them to run their own business and, at times, make their own mistakes." Leaders who can't let go usually wind up micromanaging, overfunctioning, and destroying trust. In essence, a leader who behaves like this is saying to her subordinates, "This would be a great relationship if it weren't for you." To help my clients learn how to let go I ask them to:

- *Identify the source.* Who is it that you don't trust? Is the problem really about everyone else, or is it about you?

157

- *Realize that we often see things in others before we see them in ourselves.* It's happened more than once that a leader may have a particularly negative opinion about the behavior of a team member, only to realize through therapy that he is guilty of the same behavior. I had asked Aadya, an up-and-coming manager in India, to talk to me about her family, and she started telling me about her sister. She described her sister as domineering, doing things for Aadya she didn't need done for her and giving her advice she didn't ask for. The thing is, her team complained that Aadya did the same thing. She could have been describing herself.

- *Acknowledge the blue badge.* At Microsoft everyone wears a blue security badge. Whenever conflict arises, we are encouraged to remember that despite our different departments and responsibilities, being a part of Microsoft, and caring about the future of the company, is our strongest, most common bond. Every manager would do well to remind his team of their common bonds from time to time.

- *Is this a new or old problem?* Are you repeating old behaviors? Do you have a history of not being able to let go? I have known one leader for many years who intellectually understands the need to let go and empower his team. Emotionally, though, he is unable to do so. His team is so well trained that even when asked to prepare a report for a meeting they will not do so because they assume (rightly) that investing time in the report will be a wasted investment since Martin will just do it over his way. They don't feel trusted and Martin is constantly overfunctioning in an effort to deliver on the team's objectives.

Occasionally I have been brought in to mediate a conflict between two individuals that has caused a complete breakdown in trust between leaders and their teams. Mary and Johanna were asked to work with me when their relationship reached an all-time low. Their antipathy and mistrust had infected their teams. Mary led a developer team and Johanna a marketing team. Johanna thought that Mary ignored her team's requirements, Mary thought that Johanna's team didn't deliver. I suggested we have three sessions to identify the problem, agree on a solution and move forward. In our first session it was clear neither was willing to listen to the other. They clung to their relative positions: "You never listen." "You never deliver." To break the impasse I asked each to frame the problem from the other's perspective—to use their mindreading skills to try and identify the real cause of the problem. After some grumbling they agreed to try. Johanna guessed that Mary's team was under a tremendous pressure to deliver and Mary must have to have a single-minded focus to achieve these deadlines. Mary mused that Johanna's marketing team might experience severe problems if Mary's team didn't communicate the features of the software they were developing. Through this communication each began to appreciate the needs of the other and soften their stance. Over the course of the next two sessions they talked more about their respective working styles. Mary was much more private and business-focused, Johanna more gregarious and relationship-focused. But they both agreed they cared for and invested a huge amount of time in their respective teams. Over the course of our work together they spent part of a day shadowing one another to gain more of an appreciation of each other's style and the needs of their respective teams. For Johanna and Mary, trust didn't emerge overnight, but by taking the time to acknowledge their similarities and differences, they could begin to build a relationship where trust could grow.

Of course there are always limits to how far a leader should go to accommodate or promote different working styles and approaches. I often think of one leader who told me, "People want to be led by a strong leader. If there are some who will not come with you, you need to minimize their impact or get them off the team." He's right. Accommodating mediocrity or dissension can also destroy trust. For example, if you need your people to be self-directed problem solvers, the last thing you want is a person who needs to run things by you all the time. Lack of confidence and need for approval is a style you cannot accommodate. Leaders have to find a way to give team members lots of opportunity to make mistakes and find their common ground, while still allowing them to trust that you will preserve the integrity, efficiency, and credibility of the team as a whole.

Let Go of the Past

The third way a leader can restore trust between himself and his team is let go of the past. In chapter 2 I described how corporate life events can challenge a leader's ability to adapt and regain his equilibrium. A promotion or change in responsibility at work has been found to be a significant life event. Managers in Asia, the Americas, and Europe have complained that getting that much longed-for promotion is second only to dealing with a divorce in terms of challenging experiences.[12] Steve Newhall, who conducted this research, states that after the euphoria of getting the new position dies down, "the reality hits home: you are on your own, unsure of what is really expected of you, missing aspects of your previous role that you have finally mastered." To cope, many of these managers try to go back to what they did before, being "one of the gang" and trying to be friends with subordinates, or taking on aspects of their directs' jobs. All of these behaviors break down trust. One trap associated with the newly promoted leader is the Impostor Syndrome, where a leader lives in constant fear of being found to be a fraud who shouldn't have been promoted in the first place. This lack of self-confidence impacts trust as subordinates tire of constantly having to reassure these leaders of their ability and begin to doubt they can work with someone so insecure.

The following examples illustrate how and why some of my clients had to let go of the past to restore trust in the present.

I first met Barak during an offsite I had been invited to attend to help improve trust among members of his team. By the time the offsite took place the team was in crisis and relationships were at an all-time low. Results from a web-based survey conducted prior to the offsite indicated few people on his team trusted one another, and even fewer felt "deeply invested in one another's success." Among the exercises I conducted to get to the source of their problem was Team Geometry. The exercise proved that many members of the team had a very difficult time trusting Barak. His teammates regularly placed him as far away from the center of their circle as possible. After the offsite Barak asked me to work with him further to help him understand why his behavior caused so much distrust. Over the course of several sessions a number of things became abundantly clear. He managed up to his boss extremely well and his direct reports loved him. The problem was with his peers. He didn't trust them and they didn't trust him. A lot of this hostility was caused by Barak's belief that he had to be the alpha dog—that he was in competition with his teammates for recognition and career advancement.

Consequently in his relationships with these people he came across as cold and distant, even intimidating. His need to be the best pointed toward the Impostor Syndrome. He demonstrated several of the classic symptoms of this particular confidence trap—his need to be the favorite with his teachers, his struggle with perfectionism and constant need for reassurance and approval from his boss. All of these realizations helped him begin to soften his approach, yet throughout he still struggled with trust. The breakthrough came when we talked more about his childhood. Barak's father had repeatedly told his son "people will always let you down." Barak internalized this script and approached many of his relationships with the expectation that people would fail him. Over time we worked on helping him let go of the harmful twisted thinking his father had ingrained in him, freeing him to pursue healthier relationships. Barak eventually left his group to join another division where he reinvented himself as someone who was ambitious and self-directed, but who worked extremely well with his peers, who could trust and be trusted.

In this case, Short Term Corporate Therapy allowed Barak to become aware of what drove his behavior and to choose a new path—to open a new "trust account," if you will. His problems didn't go away; he simply became more adept at managing them so they could no longer manage him.

It's not just individuals who cling to the past. Teams can be guilty of it, too. Joan had been with Microsoft for only a short time when I was asked by the human resources department to help with her "onboarding" process. For many, joining a company like Microsoft can be a bewildering experience—the huge scale, frantic pace, and bizarre language (every company seems to have its own vocabulary and acronyms). The first six months at Microsoft have been likened to drinking tequila from a fire hose! Once you reach that six-month milestone things get considerably easier; the challenge is getting to that milestone. When I met Joan she was finding it tough going. She'd made some missteps with her new team, some minor, others more significant. We agreed I'd meet with each member of her team to "take the pulse" and gain a deeper understanding as to how they might all work more effectively together. By the time I had finished these meetings it was clear that the team didn't trust Joan. They felt she didn't listen, and, more importantly, that she had let them down by promising more resources and then failing to live up to her word. She was reticent to share information and had a tendency to come across as somewhat dictatorial. While this feedback seemed significant I didn't feel I was hearing the whole story. I wasn't convinced that if Joan changed her behavior the team would forgive and forget. By learning more about the history of the team, however, I was able to get to the heart of the problem. A Microsoft veteran had created the business and brought this particular team together. He had been a charismatic, popular leader who was also very hands-off, allowing members of the team to have considerable autonomy. He subsequently made way for Joan, who was hired to take the business to the next level. But even barring Joan's early mistakes, she'd never gain the team's trust until it let go of its attachment to the previous leader and stopped blaming Joan for his departure. Similarly, Joan had to believe that the team could help her and the business be successful. In order to facilitate letting go of the past, the team took part in an offsite to honestly discuss their misgivings. I started the offsite by reviewing a "report card" I had put together based on my one-on-one discussions. I gave the team an "F" for trust. (If there is one thing people in Microsoft hate, it is failing and I knew this grade would shock them into taking the issue of trust seriously.) Over the course of the day team members told Joan how her behavior caused doubt and distrust and Joan described what she needed from the team. We finished by creating a blueprint that would outline what they would do differently following the offsite.

BREAKING THE BONDS OF TRUST

Galford and Drapeau's list of the common enemies of trust includes almost any act of bad management, from inconsistency to underperformance to tolerating rumors. There are several, however, that I have witnessed and feel deserve mention:

- *Overfunctioning.* As discussed in chapter 3, overfunctioning is one of the traps leaders fall into when they lack confidence. This behavior causes others to underfunction because they don't feel trusted to make good decisions.
- *Snooping.* Being overly inquisitive or nosy is a softer form of overfunctioning and often directly related to problems with letting go of the past. People who take on new leadership roles often miss parts of their old job, like seeing customers, working with partners, having time to think or strategize. Instead they are mired in an endless cycle of meetings, and feel overly responsible for managing the needs of the people in their business. To compensate they take an unhealthy interest in what is happening in their organization, inquiring about details or getting involved at levels that they would normally delegate. The people whose job it is to handle these details or projects often interpret their boss's hovering as a lack of trust in their abilities. "If he trusted me he wouldn't go around me to talk to my directs to find out what they are up to," or, "If she trusted me I wouldn't have to take her on my customer calls."
- *Hoarding information.* Many leaders forget to communicate where they are spending their time. As one direct said to her manager in

one of my sessions, "People on your team want to hear what you're up to, what others in the business are up to, to feel a connection with you and trust that you're doing your best for them." A leader must always remember that everything he does, and everything he doesn't do, communicates a message. By not sharing information about what he's doing he's sending the message that his team doesn't matter.

- *Assume positive intent.* At the start of every offsite or meeting I facilitate I present my Ten Laws of Effective Meetings, one of which is "Assume Positive Intent." All too often we make a judgment about a colleague's intentions based on how they make us feel. We feel criticized so we assume they meant to criticize us; we feel hurt so we imagine they meant to hurt us. This tendency to respond emotionally creates cynicism and distrust. By assuming positive intent leaders can maintain their focus on the problem to be solved. Some clients find this process difficult, so I advise them to reflect on what they have to lose if they change their mind about someone. Is their pride or self-esteem at risk if they accept that another person may not have intended any harm? Does it make them vulnerable? I also ask them to conduct a Reality Check—the process I described in chapter 3 that helps ascertain which beliefs are worth preserving—to put some distance between themselves and their emotions. There are, of course, occasions where it's important to share how you feel, for example: "Bob, when you say my team is difficult to get along with I can't help but feel criticized." Bob may respond that that wasn't his intent, or that he does indeed feel critical of your behavior or performance. The important part of this dialogue is to ensure that Bob understands how you feel and that he has a chance to explain in more detail, or in a more effective fashion, the reasons for his comments. Keeping this dialogue going with all of your teammates, subordinates, and superiors is key to being trusted.

THE GEOMETRY OF TRUST

Every relationship has its own combination of lines, angles, and arcs that can facilitate or hinder trust. The simplest form of relational geometry is the straight line between two people. This structure is the basis for any open, honest, and trusting relationship. Circles also help facilitate communication and honesty. In my work with teams I often seat everyone in a circle to ensure they can see one another. This helps focus communication between people and prevents them from talking about others on the team in the third person. I am always surprised at how many meetings take place using the traditional boardroom format, the rectangle, even if they're not in a boardroom. This seating arrangement means most people in the room cannot see one another. As a rule of thumb, if people can't see you then they are probably not listening to you, either.

The third shape relationships can take is the triangle. A triangular relationship involves a person who gossips to a colleague about the behavior of a coworker, and it's a serious problem in a lot of work environments. We all complain about people from time to time, but unresolved conflict, played out by triangling others, is one of the most potent enemies of trust. When I shadow my clients in their work environments, there are two forms of triangling I watch for. One is a version of the flying monkeys example we saw in chapter 4. Often, when my client is a manager, I'll witness a meeting in which someone on the team complains about the behavior of a colleague. The complainant's goal is to get my client to take his side by triangling her into the problem. The manager usually reassures the complainant that she will meet with the other person and get to the bottom of the matter. But now the manager has been triangled into an alliance with the disgruntled direct report, hurting her chances of keeping an objective eye on the situation. Whenever I see this happen I urge the manager to ask if the "complainant" has directly spoken to the "defendant." In most cases they haven't spoken. Only as a last resort should a leader get directly involved in trying to resolve the issue, and then only as a mediator in a three-way meeting.

Triangling can happen during team meetings, too, and be particularly destructive. Consider this example. Bill and Mary have a fraught relationship; neither trusts the other. They are disagreeing over budget figures in a meeting. After several minutes of holding up the meeting with their bickering, Bill turns to his friend and coworker John and asks, "You agree with my figures, don't you, John?" John replies, "They seem reasonable." Bill has now successfully triangled John into his disagreement with Mary. John then asks Barb, "You see where I'm coming from, right, Barb?" As more triangles are formed, Mary becomes more isolated.

A leader cannot take sides. The most important thing to remember if you see triangling begin in a meeting is to focus on the problem—in this case reconciling the budget figures—not the emotional issue between people. That problem can wait until after the meeting. In this example, whoever is heading up this meeting should refocus the team's attention on the figures and ask Mary and Bill to get together after the meeting and resolve their personal problem. To do otherwise is to become mired in an escalating series of triangles.[13]

There is one other issue that can hinder a leader's success, and it directly influences trust. It's one of the issues leaders are most uncomfortable talking about: power.

TRUST: THINGS TO THINK ABOUT

Trust is the glue of any properly functioning organization, business, or team. It is a quality every leader needs to build and safeguard by managing the expectations of himself and others, acknowledging and accepting differences in working style, temperament, and personality, and by letting go of the past.

The following questions will help you gain more insight into how to build trust, how to maintain it, and how to avoid the enemies of trust.

1. Draw a circle and place a dot in the center to represent yourself. Next, position everyone you work with according to how much or how little trust exists between you and them. Overall, do you have a trusting relationship with the majority of your organization or did most of your team wind up near or outside the edge of your circle?

2. Have you established expectations within your team? Do you know what they need from you to be successful? Have you shared with them what you need? How might you fix these expectations into the fabric of your business so they aren't forgotten or ignored?

3. Who do you trust least on your team? Have you thought about why? Do you see any parallels between their behavior and your own?

4. Do you assume positive intent when someone criticizes you or your business?

5. Do you find your self being pulled into triangles by your directs? How can you stop this happening? Do you have a triangular

relationship with anyone on your team? How could you change the shape of this relationship?

6. Have you hired strong people but find it hard to trust them because they have a different approach to you? Is your way really the only way? What are you losing by not empowering them; what is the business losing?

6

Power and Ambition

Do You Want to Be Feared or Loved?

"No one can lead who does not first acquire power, and no leader can be great who does not know how to use power."[1]

THE SHOCKING TRUTH ABOUT POWER

Imagine. You are sitting in a well-appointed research laboratory in front of a piece of equipment called a shock generator. You have volunteered for an experiment on memory and learning at prestigious Yale University. You and a fellow volunteer draw straws. You will play the role of the teacher, and the other participant will be the learner. You watch as the learner is strapped into a chair, which is linked to the shock generator located in another room by two cuffs affixed to his arms. The research scientist in charge of the experiment tells you both, "Although the shocks can be painful, they cause no permanent damage."[2] You are led to the room where the shock generator sits and are instructed to sit down and await further instructions. You cannot see the learner, but you can communicate with one another via an intercom device. You notice that the front panel of the generator has a number of switches labeled from left to right, "mild shock" to "intense shock" all the way to "xxx." You are given a list of questions to ask your partner, the learner. Should he get an answer wrong you are to administer a shock by depressing one of the levers on the front of the generator. Should the learner make another mistake you are to give a more severe shock. You learn that the shocks range from a mild but painful 15 volts to a potentially fatal 450 volts. The experiment begins and for the first five minutes all goes smoothly—you ask a question and the learner answers correctly. Then you ask another question and for the first time the learner makes a mistake. The researcher instructs you to punish the learner by giving him a shock of 45 volts. You hesitate, but the researcher reminds you of your commitment to the research. He adds, "The experiment requires you that you continue. You have no other choice, you must go on." In the face of this pressure, what do you do?

You may have already recognized this scenario as one of the most powerful research studies in the history of experimental psychology—Stanley Milgram's groundbreaking 1961 study on obedience. The "learner" was an actor pretending to be shocked. During the study he would scream and beg to be let out of the experiment as the shocks continued to be administered. Prior to the study Milgram asked a sample of psychiatrists what proportion of the participants they thought would shock the learner. The psychiatrists predicted that only 4 percent would go up to 300 volts and that only a pathological fringe of approximately one in a thousand would administer the highest shock on the generator. After the study, Milgram found that 65 percent of ordinary citizens administered the maximum shock possible—450 volts, enough to kill a human being. Why? Because an authority figure commanded them to. Even more surprising, not one participant refused to follow orders until they thought they were being told to deliver 300 or more volts.

I show a video of Milgram's experiment to leaders and teams I work with when I want to provoke a discussion about power. It's an effective way to introduce the concept. Perhaps the horrific peek into the human heart provided by Stanley Milgram explains why so many leaders are reluctant to discuss the concept of power or even acknowledge that they have it. They fear that wanting power makes them brutal or callous. They wonder if it will put them in a Machiavellian position of having to choose whether to be loved or feared—and most people want to be loved. Unfortunately, being a good leader means sometimes not being loved. On the other hand, people will more likely love us if we are unafraid of power and use it well.

So how do we get people to follow us without resorting to threats and punishment? How do we stop ourselves from succumbing to the more extreme consequences of having power? By getting people to admire our ideals, to share our values and beliefs, and to want what we want. As Joseph Nye writes in his book *Soft Power*,[3] "If a leader represents values that others want to follow, it will cost less to lead." Most executives realize instinctively that their power depends more on employee buy-in than on threats or sanctions.[4] They have to be credible and inspire confidence. It is not enough simply to be in command. A leader has to *feel* in command.[5] In this chapter we'll first consider a framework from which to understand the different types of power a leader has at his disposal. Second, we'll explore some of the most common power-related problems I see in my practice. Finally, we'll look at ambition, because whereas power is the drive for success, ambition provides the roadmap or focus of that success.

TYPES OF POWER

The framework I use to describe the different types of power available to managers and leaders was developed by John French and Bertram Raven in the late 1950s.[6] It is a rather remarkable model that has stood the test of time, providing a reliable and valid method of understanding the cause and effect of power. The model divides power into five different forms:

1. *Reward power.* A leader has the authority to distribute rewards, for example, financial bonuses, stock awards, performance review grades, and promotions. It is also true that a leader can withhold rewards as a punishment for performance-related issues or non-compliance.

2. *Coercive power.* A leader using coercive power has made it clear that employees or teammates can be punished, perhaps with censure, demotion, or a transfer to another business. People working under a coercive leader are not motivated by ambition or the love of their job, but by fear.

3. *Legitimate or role power.* This type of power stems from a leader's job title. Depending on your level in the organization, you might have the power to hire and fire employees; to reorganize your business, division or team; or to decide changes in strategy.

4. *Expert power.* A leader who has this type of power is eager to share his experience, skills, and talents with others. He freely offers technical suggestions, advice, or extra training to anyone who wants it. It is a power that is based on knowledge and skill.

5. *Referent power.* This power is derived from the relationships we build and the affiliations we create. The person with referent power is self-aware. She has a flexible interpersonal style, clear boundaries, and a secure attachment.

Many leaders feel limited in their ability to influence their subordinates because they don't see themselves as charismatic. As one client told me, "I'm just not the 'rah rah' kind of guy; I'm not comfortable getting up and thumping the table." This perception is common—the role models for many leaders are the ebullient, magnetic characters like Steve Jobs, Richard Branson, or the Microsoft CEO himself, Steve Ballmer. But as I tell my clients, what is most important is to acknowledge your expertise, where you add value to the business, and to be open and honest, sincere and trustworthy. By sharing your beliefs and expressing confidence that your goals will be achieved, any leader, regardless of his or her personality type, can lead and motivate employees.

SOFT POWER AND HARD POWER

The five types of power just described fit nicely into a more recent power grid developed by Joseph Nye, who was the Assistant Secretary of Defense for the Clinton administration. Nye proposes that we break power into two types—hard and soft. Hard power employs the use of threats, coercion, or sanctions to achieve one's goals, and soft power is "the ability to get what you want through attraction rather than coercion." Historically, hard power was suitable for business leaders. Yet today, by virtue of working with faxes, the Internet, telephones, and satellite offices, we have fewer opportunities to see or get to know the people we're supposed to manage and influence. That's why harnessing soft power has become crucial to being a good leader in this century.

When Milgram coerced unwitting test subjects to shock another human being, he discovered that proximity to power was a key determinant of obedience. The further away the teacher was from the authority figure, who might be in another room or on the telephone, the less likely he or she was to follow the instructions to shock the learner. The implications for a leader who runs an international business, who has global business partners, or even one who wants to influence a different division in the organization are clear. We cannot, in most instances, influence someone who is situated halfway across the globe through force or hard power. It's hard enough to influence people working halfway down the hall. In chapter 2 I talked about a team in India who were frustrated by their inability to attract investment from headquarters in the United States. Since they had no hard power, they discovered they had to use their soft power to make themselves as attractive as possible to the business heads who would determine whether to move key businesses from the United States to India. The leadership team could only identify their attractiveness through their value proposition and brand (quality and efficiency) to their counterparts in the United States. By using soft power they increased their attraction and credibility and created the basis for a shared dialogue. They furthered their agenda by embedding an "evangelist" in headquarters to extol the strengths of the organization.

As a company Microsoft is no stranger to soft power. Much of its business is built on relationships with external partners. Unlike IBM, there are significantly fewer salespeople selling their products and services. Microsoft relies instead on a "partner ecosystem"—a global web of relationships with small, medium, and large-scale companies, who sell, service, support, or build solutions using Microsoft products and technologies. This way the company has hundreds of thousands of salespeople to rival the scale of its competitors. They cannot force or coerce these companies to sell their software. Instead they have made the relationship attractive and economically beneficial and created a win-win for both sides.

The relationship between the five different types of power described by Raven and French and the hard and soft power model developed by Nye is illustrated in Table 6.1. The first row in the table summarizes the intent behind the behavior. With hard power, for example, the intent is to command—to seize control and use force or coercion. With soft power, the intent is to attract—to build relationships and create opportunities for cooperation. The second row categorizes the French and Raven model into hard and soft power, and the final row labels the interpersonal style associated with each category. In chapter 4 I introduced the concept of interpersonal style, where leaders choose to be passive, assertive, or aggressive. In terms of power an aggressive leader is more likely to rely on command and control—hard power—to get things done and influence others, whereas an

Table 6.1 Power Grid: Summary of Different Types of Power

	Hard	Mid-ground	Soft	Powerless
Nye's categories of power	Command, force	Valid, justifiable	Co-opt, attract	Consensus
French & Raven categories of power	Coercive,	Reward, Legitimate	Referent or Expert	
Rowley Interpersonal Styles	Aggressive	Assertive	Assertive	Passive

assertive leader relies on the referent power of his expertise and social skills. This leaves the passive leader, who in most situations will use soft power to try to achieve consensus, fearing that making the tough call will create division and conflict.

To help a leader or team identify what type of power they currently use, I show a film of the Milgram experiment, explain the power grid, and ask the following questions:

- Do you rely mainly on hard or soft power?
- Which of the five types of power do you use? (Expert, Role, Referent, etc.)
- What type of power do people on your team believe you rely on?
- What's the most frequently used type of power in your business?
- What's the most frequently used type of power in this team?

If I am working with a team I will also ask:

- What power preference does each member of this team use?

This question and answer session helps leaders become more aware of the different types of power available to them; understand the likely outcomes of using each; see how they link to their interpersonal style; and explain why they might gravitate to a particular one. This critical exercise ensures that leaders understand how their own power grid might limit or aid their impact and influence.

THE DOWNSIDE TO POWER

There are five situations in which power becomes a stumbling block:

1. When greatness is thrust upon us;
2. When we become martyrs;

3. When we have influence without authority;
4. When we are feared; and
5. When expertise bites back.

When Greatness Is Thrust upon Us

Much of what we hear and read about power, and people with power, makes it seem as though power is something everyone desires. In my experience this is not the case. A number of clients have difficulty with the power they acquire through a promotion or other change in their job. Peter was just such a client. He had become almost paralyzed by a recent promotion to vice president. A software architect, Peter was a maverick who had a reputation for being decisive and extremely innovative. However, after being promoted he became uncharacteristically ineffective and started playing things safe. As we discussed his situation it became clear that he had become intimidated by the role power of the VP position. His decisiveness had become blunted by his determination to make sure his behavior aligned with his perceptions of the role of a vice president. To regain his effectiveness, he had to rediscover what had made him so successful in the past, stop trying to please everyone, and chart his own course. Over several sessions we identified his primary fear: becoming something he wasn't in order to fulfill his new role. Peter had decided that to succeed in this position he would have to turn his back on the qualities that led to his promotion—his decisiveness, his web of trusted relationships, and his independence—and replace them with adherence to bureaucracy and to creating consensus, behaviors he wasn't good at. To get him back on the right track, I counseled him to build a high-performance team to delegate decision making down through his business. This would give him more time to use his referent power instead of role power to drive the business forward. He used referent and expert power to reestablish his authority and define his new role.

When We Become Martyrs

It's not only individuals who may have problems acting with influence or authority; whole teams can give away their power. In one case a marketing department asked if I could help them improve the effectiveness of their leadership team. One of the first things I had them do was create a metaphor for the team using parts of the body. In this exercise, I give everyone on the team a different body part—the leader of the team usually gets the head, someone else will get the brain, torso, legs, arms, and so on. Each person is then instructed to draw his or her body part as they feel it represents the team. When this team's body was finished, all eyes were drawn to the torso, which had been drawn as pierced by several arrows. As the individual who had drawn the torso explained the reason for this particular representation the discussion moved to how the team didn't feel valued for its contribution to the business; instead they felt that they were being victimized. They didn't feel valued for their contribution because as marketers they didn't directly bring in revenue. During subsequent conversations I was struck by how they had created a codependent role with the rest of the business. They had become dependent on the perceptions of others; they were difficult to get along with and hypercritical of their own abilities. Rather than go on the offensive and evangelize the role and purpose of the team, they had become defensive and allowed themselves to become martyrs.

Rather than challenge the unfavorable beliefs of the organization, they had given away their power.

When We Have Influence without Authority

Needing influence but lacking any formal role power or authority is a common problem many of my clients face working in a global business. The key to fixing this dilemma is building a credible network. Networking has become a well-established part of any executive's power base. But how do you start and who do you choose to let into your inner circle? I tell clients to identify no more than six individuals in the organization who can help them advance their agenda. The reason I limit the number is that networks take time to build and just as much time to maintain.

I urge my clients to be creative in who they choose to be part of their network. Their tendency is to include people they already know or like. But research into the real efficacy of social networks points in a different direction. For example, sociologist Emile Granovetter found that weak relationships were more helpful than more established ones in finding a new job. Only 16 percent of the people he spoke to got their jobs through contacts they saw "often," whereas 84 percent got their jobs through contacts they saw "occasionally" or "rarely." He concluded that "Weak ties are an important resource."[7] If you broadcast your needs to loose acquaintances your news has a greater chance to "escape the confining boundaries of your own social group and get into the minds of a great many people." Of course, being able to exploit these ties requires both referent power and expertise.

When We Are Feared

"I need her to be less Mount Vesuvius—she's intimidating." I'd been asked to work with a leader whose manager feedback was dismal. As I met with her directs I heard the same story time and time again. Jocelyn was extremely certain of her role and goals, and "super smart," but her lack of self-awareness and aggressive interpersonal style made her someone to fear, not love. As I watched her in action I could see that sometimes she could be supportive and encouraging, but that often she used her power to criticize and demean. She was probably one of the most complex women I have ever worked with—at times Dr. Jekyll, at others Ms. Hyde. The problem was that no one, including me, knew who was going to show up at any given moment, so her team had become paralyzed by fear. No one stood up to Jocelyn, so the team suffered from groupthink, a dysfunctional approach to decision making where no one raises concerns or voices objections, in this case for fear of incurring Jocelyn's wrath.

As I got to know her I met a woman who had huge potential, but she was harboring deep anger and despair. She had experienced a series of devastating personal tragedies, and seemed to me to have never recovered from these traumas. From my perspective she had turned her anguish into a weapon she used both on herself and others. I worked with Jocelyn and her team for several weeks but never made a breakthrough—small incremental gains would be lost in the aftermath of a harsh word or public tongue-lashing. She clung to hard power as her lifeline. I assumed that she felt by using force she could have control in at least one area of her life, and try as I might I couldn't free her of this perception. She needed to be feared. We agreed to cease our work together—this was one occasion where I couldn't gain traction to create lasting change.

WHEN EXPERTISE BITES BACK

In my experience expert power is not always benign. In some circumstances the leader with considerable intellectual horsepower can unwittingly paralyze his team, provoking feelings of inferiority and resentment. I was called in to work with one such leadership team. The presenting problem seemed pretty straightforward—the team was fragmented and worked in silos because the pressure of work forced each leader to focus more on his or her team rather than the business as a whole. My preference is always to create more of a "Board of Directors" approach to team working at the top where each leader "comes to the table" able to focus on the needs of the overall business rather than just the needs of his or her own team, department, or division. I soon found out that my initial diagnosis was wide of the mark. As I started interviewing each member of the team I heard the same story: Christopher, the leader of the business was "an intellectual giant," "the dominant force," and the "smartest person they had ever met" and this, they confided, was the cause of the problem. He was so damn smart and had such high expectations of his team that they had literally given up trying to engage in a meaningful discussion or debate with him as they always felt they would "lose" or look foolish and ill-equipped in front of their peers. To try and "quantify" this system I asked each leader to assess his or her own interpersonal style using the scale of "passive, assertive, and aggressive" I introduced in chapter 4. Most rated themselves as being assertive; falling between 10 to 12 on the scale, but this dropped significantly when they were in team meetings with Christopher. In this situation they rated themselves as being more "passive," scoring a low of between 5 or 6. On the face of it Christopher was a leader who had significant expert power but rather than using it to help members of his team develop and mature, or to think differently about their business, his strongest asset was for them a liability, a force to avoid or steer clear of. Yet the more I thought about the problem being played out between Christopher and his team the more I thought I wasn't hearing the whole story. The problem reminded me of the frequently-heard complaint in couple's therapy: "This would be a great relationship if not for him!" What I wondered was the role the direct reports played in maintaining this system of paralysis and isolation? In talking to Christopher I heard a different perspective. He was frustrated with the team for disengaging. To be sure, there were situations where the team performed well, but these were few and far between and driven by the demands of Senior Executives and not Christopher himself. I shared with Christopher the fact that his power was a factor in the inconsistent performance of his team, how people switched and became passive, but I also shared my feeling that his directs also had a role to play in maintaining this negative relationship system. "What was in it for them?" he asked. From my perspective they were able to avoid or ignore their larger responsibilities to the business, steer clear of any conflict or tension with their peers (much easier to blame everything on Christopher), and in general escape any shared accountability. To resolve the problem we decided to hold a team meeting to "out" the issues. I took the team through my "diagnosis" and pointed out it was a system they were all responsible for keeping in place. We worked on how to change the relationship pattern where the team became "passive" in their meeting together—this included a very candid discussion of what the team needed from Christopher and what he needed from them going forward. By managing expectations in this fashion the team felt more empowered to challenge Christopher and he felt less frustrated at the team's inability to engage in meaningful discussion and debate, not just with him but with each other. I also suggested that the team use the whiteboard to Brainstorm. Christopher was a whiteboard fiend and he was much more inclusive and listened more effectively when he was working at the whiteboard with people. The team also appointed a "passivity" cop to call out if the team was slipping back into old ways of relating.

AMBITION

There is a distinction to be made between power and ambition. Whereas power is the tool we use to get things done, ambition sets the direction for this achievement. It is the cornerstone on which power rests. Ambition, like power, is something we often discuss in relation to other people but that we are rarely comfortable talking about with regard to ourselves. We often disapprove of people who abuse ambition, but dismiss people who aren't "hungry" enough or have "fire in the belly." I experienced firsthand the disapproval associated with the term when I gave a talk on leadership to a group of managers in India. During my presentation I spoke about ambition. Afterward, one of the managers advised me that "ambition is a dirty word in Indian society" because it is associated with selfishness. "Far better," he said, "to use [the word] 'aspiration' instead." I've had clients in the States, too, wrinkle their nose at the mention of ambition, as though it were synonymous with "greed," "selfishness," and "cutthroat." A leader with ambition is none of these things. Rather, she realizes that ambition charts the course for future endeavors. Like power, or boundaries, or interpersonal styles, there are several categories of ambition, some more conducive to good leadership than others.

To understand the perceptions associated with ambition I conducted a survey of leaders in the United States and Canada. The results established three types of ambition—positive, narcissistic, and negative.

Positive Ambition

This type of ambition is healthy for the leader, her team, and the company. It provides a sense of intrinsic satisfaction and has a positive impact on others because it's about doing what's right. Individuals with positive ambition get excited about the difference they can make, and they want to contribute as well as learn.

Leaders with positive ambition:

- Have strong desires to achieve their goal, however large or small;
- hold in their mind a clear picture of what success looks like;
- demonstrate the tenacity to stick with their goal even in the face of great obstacles;
- prefer to be part of a large team and organization that shares the same ambition;
- feel proud of their achievements; and
- focus not only on results but on the journey, and ensure it is as fulfilling and rewarding as possible to all those involved.

Narcissistic Ambition

People with narcissistic ambition are not concerned about the consequences of achieving their goals and thus they can be destructive to others. They may often preach about their success, power and money, elevating themselves above others. This ambition is unhealthy for anyone remotely involved.

Leaders with narcissistic ambition:

- Harbor an intense desire to compete rather than cooperate;
- hear only what they want to hear and what fits with their agenda;
- are not afraid to be exploitative or political to achieve what they want;
- take flagrant risks;
- believe the ends always justify the means; and
- need to dominate subordinates.

Probably the most powerful example of narcissistic ambition is Jeffrey Skilling of Enron. In his book *The Smartest Guys in the Room* Peter Elkind observes that "ambition ran amok" in the company and that, over time, "[Skilling's] arrogance hardened, and he became so sure that he was the smartest guy in the room that anyone who disagreed with him was summarily dismissed as just not bright enough to 'get it.'" Not only did he have a dysfunctional approach to ambition, his need for "hard power" made him unwilling and unable to curb his excessive appetites.

Negative Ambition

This type of ambition is externally oriented. Individuals with negative ambition often try to prove something to themselves and others using an organization's or society's definitions of success as their guide. This may do little or no harm to others but may be detrimental to the individual, as they may achieve no sense of internal gratification.

Leaders with negative ambition:

- Have low self-esteem and their success is seen as a means to stave off feelings of inadequacy;
- feel hollow despite their success; and
- gravitate to areas where they can succeed but often have little feeling or passion for the work.

WHERE DOES AMBITION COME FROM?

Like many personality attributes, ambition is the sum of both nature and nurture—a combination of genetic disposition, parenting, personality, and environment.

For young people, ambition is a process of social comparison—kids want to be bigger, stronger, and taller. As we get older our ambitions change. We want success in school, our personal life, and our jobs. As we mature, however, it's important to develop realistic expectations around our ambitions. A study into the relationship between depression and ambition reveals important data relevant to ambition. Until the 1980s, researchers had proposed that gifted or talented children were less emotionally resilient than their less talented peers. To test this theory, Joan Freeman, a British psychologist, decided to analyze the rates of depression in a population of children who belonged to the Society for Gifted Children.[8] At the time of the study anyone could nominate their child to become a member of the society. Freeman found that children whose ambition matched their talents were significantly happier and more adjusted than those children who had been labeled as gifted but who were not. It's crucial that managers or leaders have realistic ambitions that stretch their abilities. Unrealistic expectations can lead to frustrated ambition, stress, and burnout.

CAN AMBITION CHANGE OVER TIME?

Our ambition can change. For many, getting married or starting a family has a significant impact on their ambition. As one client told me, "Having a family changes a lot of stuff—my principal ambition now is to provide security for my family for their future. This does not, ironically, lessen the desire to climb the corporate ladder; it just makes everything a little more important."

There are also those whose ambition is to be satisfied with where they are. What happens if you have reached the top of your own corporate ladder? I have counselled many leaders who are very happy with their job, but feel a tremendous pressure to climb to the next rung. Yet they know that this would be a step too far for them. It's okay to say no to others' ambition for you and recognize that it's what you want that is most important.

EMBRACING POWER AND FRAMING AMBITION

When working with my clients I try to demonstrate that power is much more than the inexorable slide into corruption, or a choice between the extremes of being loved or feared. It goes to the heart of who you are as a leader, and who you are as a person. As the historian Robert Caro observes, "When a leader gets enough power, when he doesn't need anybody anymore—when he's president of the United States or a CEO of a major corporation—then we see how he always wanted to treat people, and we can also see—by watching what he does with his power—what he wanted to accomplish all along." Not all of us become CEOs or president of our country, but all of us have to make peace with power and ambition. Joseph Campbell, the teacher and historian, put these two forces in context when he advised his students to follow their bliss. "If you do follow your bliss you put yourself on a kind of track that has been there all the while, waiting for you, and the life that you ought to be living is the one you are living. When you can see that, you begin to meet people who are in your field of bliss, and they open doors to you. I say, follow your bliss and don't be afraid, and doors will open where you didn't know they were going to be."[9] What Campbell means is that ambition, true ambition, means identifying and remaining true to the pursuit that ignites our passion. To follow our bliss is to embrace power and pursue our dreams and ambitions. Power and ambition are two sides of the same coin that need to be kept in balance. Some of my clients have become consumed by what psychiatrists call monomania—an obsessive interest in one area. In their case it is work. As one general manager in the United Kingdom confided, working at Microsoft is "like a drug—you keep chasing it." This type of obsessional focus can result in physical and emotional burnout and increases the likelihood of a reliance on coercion and force to get things done, as the need to achieve outweighs the need to think critically. The General Manager's comments were very interesting to me as they provided an insight both into the culture of Microsoft and the temperament of the leaders who work there. Many leaders in the company are at risk of what I call "neurotic ambition," an addiction to the "rush" of getting things done to the exclusion of all else in their lives, and an overreliance on achievement at work to bolster self-esteem. These characteristics suggest a tendency toward an addictive personality and to test out my theory I reviewed the symptomatology for addictive behavior in the DSM IV (The Diagnostic and Statistical Manual used by psychiatrists to determine a diagnosis)[10] and shared my findings with some of my clients. By substituting "work" for substance abuse the following criteria emerged.

- Work often taken in larger amounts or over a longer period than the person intended.
- Persistent desire to reduce the amount of time spent at work or thinking about work, or one or more unsuccessful efforts to cut down or control working hours.
- A great deal of time spent in work or work-related activities even when away from the workplace—many Leaders I spoke to talked about being physically present at home but intellectually and emotionally being still at work.
- Important personal, social, or recreational activities given up or reduced because of attitude toward work.
- Marked tolerance: need for markedly increased amounts of pressure in order to achieve "intoxication" or desired effect.

The criteria used to assess the "severity" of work addiction are based on the degree of impairment caused by the above behaviors. A "mild" case would exist if the leader experiences mild impairment in occupational functioning or in usual social relationships with others. More severe cases would be indicated if the symptoms have a marked effect on the health and social and emotional functioning of the leader. Risk factors for work addiction or workoholism include "compulsive tendencies" (*I always seem to be in a hurry and racing against the clock; I overly commit myself*); control (*I get impatient when I have to wait too long for someone else; I get angry when people don't meet my standards*), an inability to delegate (*I prefer to do things by myself*); self-worth (*I get upset with myself if I make a small mistake; I put myself under pressure with self-imposed deadlines*), and impaired communication and self-absorption (*I forget, ignore, or minimize birthdays; I spend more time working than socializing with friends*). The causes of work addiction are many and varied and whilst many blame the culture of an organization the roots lie in our attitudes toward, and beliefs about ourselves. I remember a major concern we investigated during the TOYA study was the emotional risk of competitive sport for young people, in particular the effect competition could have upon the relationship between the child and his or her parents. We discovered that competitive sport is neither good nor bad—sport highlighted problems that already existed in the family system—it didn't cause them. Work is similar—in the majority of cases it doesn't cause many of the problems we experience; it highlights a predisposition to addiction, self-doubt, an inability to trust, or neurotic ambition. Some leaders work to fill an emptiness in themselves they don't want to acknowledge; others work long hours because they don't want to go home; and some invest their sense of self in what they do. The more they work the better they feel about themselves. Whatever the cause of work addiction, the long-term prognosis of these behaviors is burnout.

Based upon this work I was invited to run a series of workshops on Burnout. I called the series "Taming the Hungry Ghost." In Buddhist philosophy the different forms of human existence are captured in a wheel or circle of life. One of the most vividly drawn metaphors on the wheel is the "Hungry Ghosts." These phantomlike creatures with withered limbs, bloated bellies, and long thin necks have insatiable appetites they cannot fulfill. The "ghosts" speak directly to what can happen when a leader loses her equilibrium and begins a downward spiral of overachievement, perfectionism, exhaustion, and ultimately emptiness. The hungry ghosts are what happens on the wheel of corporate life when you burnout. The workshops only met with moderate success; my message of personal accountability fell on largely deaf ears—people didn't want to hear that they had to make a choice—to balance the demands of work with other pursuits and interests in their lives—most wanted to vent and blame something or someone for the pressure and lack of balance in their lives.

I still contend that leaders must be open about their ambitions asking themselves: What drives me? What gets me out of bed in the morning? What values underpin my ambition and how are these aligned with the values of the organization? Another crucial question to ask and answer is, to whom does your ambition belong? Are you driving your ambition, or are you acting out your parents' hopes and aspirations? To what degree have you absorbed what I call "expected ambition," the desire to climb the corporate ladder, or to follow the herd at the expense of your own path or journey?

And what of power? I'd like to think if Machiavelli were writing his treatise on power for the prince today he would offer a third alternative to being feared or loved. He might propose that soft power, characterized by sharing expertise, cooperation, and attraction might be a better alternative to the modern-day "prince" managing a global business.

POWER: THINGS TO THINK ABOUT

To be credible and inspire confidence it's not enough to simply be in command. Leaders have to feel in command. To achieve this they need to be comfortable wielding the different types of power at their disposal and avoid letting their ambition cloud their judgment or decision making.

Use the following questions to learn more about your relationship with power.

1. Which type of power do you find yourself using most often in your business or team—role, reward, coercive, expert, or referent power? Which do you hardly ever use? Why?

2. What is the most frequently used type of power in your business? How does this affect the quality of attachment people lower down in the organization may have with the leadership?

3. Are there situations you face where you feel powerless? What happens? How might you get your power back?

4. How might you use expert power more effectively? How would you define your expertise?

5. What is your ambition? Has it stayed the same for some time or has it changed? When or how did it change?

7

Be Your Own Therapist

"Our mastery of work helps us to define ourselves and in the best of circumstances, adds to our self-worth. Perhaps the genius of humankind is to make a pleasure out of necessity. The psychological, intellectual, or physical stretch we feel when we are full-out at work contributes mightily to that pleasure."

—Ethel Person[1]

DO IT YOURSELF STCT

Throughout the course of this book we have examined how many common emotional and behavior problems can rob people of the pleasure psychotherapist Ethel Person describes. These problems can happen to anyone, at any time, and be triggered by any number of different events or experiences, large and small. I've revealed how Short Term Corporate Therapy has helped hundreds of men and women to work through those problems and reinvigorate their careers and their attitudes toward work. But let's say your company doesn't provide in-house therapy, or for whatever reason you're not ready to start working with a professional therapist. How can you protect yourself from tumbling into one of the six confidence traps, or increase your self-awareness to reduce the size of your blind spots? What can you do to maintain a healthy perspective regarding power and ambition? How do you maintain the trust of your employees or team? And how can you be sure you are living in accordance with your beliefs? In this final chapter you'll learn the five steps you can take to become your own therapist:

1. Know when to start.
2. Assess the problem.
3. Make a plan.
4. Create your own 50-minute hour.
5. Enlist support.

While there is no substitute for the education and experience of a properly trained analyst or psychotherapist, these steps will enable you to bolster your beliefs, maximize your confidence, self-awareness, and trust, and enjoy your power so you can maintain the three essentials of mental health in the workplace—self-actualization, subjective well-being, and resilience.

Know When to Start

We've discussed a number of ways we can figure out the root of our problems, but how do you know when to employ these techniques? Microsoft believes in feedback, which means managers are constantly being forced to take stock of what they're doing right and what could use some fine-tuning. All managers take part in a midyear career discussion with their bosses to identify problematic behaviors, and all of their direct reports have the opportunity to rate their performance.

The company also conducts a mandatory poll that assesses and benchmarks the health and capability of the company, the leadership, and their teams. But despite all of these opportunities for feedback, many people still don't realize they need help until they hit a speed bump in their career. These bumps occur most often during or after one of the corporate life events I described earlier, such as a promotion that taxes a leader's capability, a reorganization that creates an awkward relationship with a senior executive, or a change in strategy or shift in focus that provokes the realization they don't believe in what they are doing. Any change can trigger a psychological landmine with the potential to blow up the smoothest career path. Therefore, when change occurs it is important to reflect on how the experience makes you feel about yourself and what doubts or fears have surfaced, and determine whether the "critic" is at risk of taking up permanent residence.

A more subtle sign that it's time for a little STCT is if you're experiencing a general feeling of unhappiness. Many clients come to see me because they are unhappy with who they are, where they are in the corporate food chain, and what they are doing or why they are doing it. Sometimes clients find that despite their best efforts they can no longer outrun the ghosts from their past—parental attitudes about success or failure, shame and guilt, fear and fraud. Consider for a moment. Are you happy? Are you the person you thought you would become, doing the job you always wanted? Your answer matters greatly to your mental health. Happiness and resilience are closely aligned. Studies have shown that after controlling for demographic variables such as income and education, and health behaviors such as drinking and smoking, happy people live significantly longer and are less likely to suffer serious injury or impairment.[2]

The question often takes my clients by surprise. After thinking about it they may respond with a qualified yes, but I always leave these conversations disappointed. Too many people simply don't expect to be happy at work. Yet happiness is a critical success factor for confidence. It affects how we feel physically, how we respond to challenges and new opportunities and whether we are pulled down by our inner critic or affirmed by our inner coach. If you cannot answer the question "Are you happy at work?" with a resounding "Yes," it's time to make some changes.

Assess the Problem

Once you know that something isn't working for you, it's time to determine what that something is. The first place to check is your belief system, because nine times out of ten that's where the problem lies. Are you leading your business or team in accordance with your beliefs or do they conflict with the culture of your organization? Do your subordinates know how your beliefs relate to vision and strategy? You can identify your beliefs using the template in the appendix.

The third-person narrative exercise, in which you shadow yourself for a day and describe what you see, is also a great way to assess how your behavior might be hurting your performance. For this exercise to provide meaningful data it's important to choose a day when you have a variety of meetings and interactions with others, for example, a series of team and one-on-one meetings and interaction with your customers. When you have completed your narrative, look over what you have written and try and see if there are any patterns or discontinuities. A pattern is any consistent behavior you notice occurring across situations—for example you may notice you have a tendency to be passive, or maybe you have a tendency to mind read before meetings. A discontinuity is when your behavior changes significantly from one situation to the next. For example, you may have a much more positive behavioral signature when working with customers than with your own directs or colleagues. The question to answer, then, is why? And once you know that answer, you can work to carry the style you use with your customers over to the people in your organization, business, or team.

You might also want to review the items in Leadership 360 in the appendix to help identify where you might need help. The more feedback you receive the more insight you will have about where you need to focus, so whenever possible get feedback from other people to assess the accuracy of your self-diagnosis. The most important reminder I can give you during this stage is to be ready to hear the worst. You might not like to admit that you are intimidated by people in senior positions, that you give away your power, or that you come across as someone who is hard to trust. But without this level of honesty it's doubtful you will make progress in working through your problem. It's also important to avoid blaming or scapegoating others for your current situation. To successfully get over your career speed bump you have to be as objective as possible about what is driving your behavior. Finally, you need to be prepared to do whatever it takes to open yourself up to new ways of experiencing yourself and others. This often means letting go of thoughts, beliefs, and behaviors you may be attached to.

Change is hard, and we all have a tendency to cling to what we know, even if it is causing us unhappiness or distress. That's why it is important to create a plan that will mobilize our resources and focus our attention.

Make a Plan

I make every one of my clients develop a plan that covers the duration of our work together. STCT works because it focuses on identifying the problem, generating solutions, and then providing opportunities to change. To help you formulate your plan I have reproduced the Development Blueprint in the appendix. The key questions to answer are:

- What is the behavior you want to improve? Is it related to low self-confidence or trust, or an unhealthy attitude toward power or ambition? Or is your difficulty caused by a dysfunctional interpersonal style? Be specific.
- What are the roots of the problem you are trying to solve? For example, are you struggling with a remnant of your childhood, or does the problem stem from a more recent experience? Is it about your relationship with others or the relationship you have with yourself?
- What will success look like 30 days from now? 60 days from now? 90 days from now? I often ask my clients, "If we were to meet in three months what would we be celebrating? What would you have accomplished? What would I notice is different about you?" Be as specific as possible regarding your future accomplishments, and be realistic.

*Create Your Own 50-Minute Hour**

One of the many advantages of psychotherapy is that it provides an opportunity for us to step out of our normal routine. Every week we get the opportunity to talk about our hopes, dreams, fears, and disappointments with a nonjudgmental person who can point out

---

* The 50-minute hour is the time most psychotherapists, analysts, or counselors spend with each client. The "extra" 10 minutes is available for writing up notes, preparing for the next client, and managing one's own emotional state.

inconsistencies in our behavior, identify unrealistic expectations or beliefs, show us how we are getting in our own way, and suggest ways we can change. While my clients are working with me they have our weekly meetings and homework to keep them focused. The problem is that, left to their own devices, most leaders rarely carve out time for themselves for thought and reflection. I often ask my clients to review their calendar and identify where they are spending their time. One European vice president discovered he was spending over 70 percent in his one-on-one meetings with his directs, 10 percent on travel, 10 percent meeting with his leadership team, and the remaining 10 percent on e-mail. I don't think Joost was atypical. Most leaders are caught up with accomplishing everything that needs to get done, rather than reflecting on their business, behavior, or performance. In other words, they are so enmeshed in *doing* that they don't allow themselves to just *be*. Taking time out is in and of itself an important development activity.

How else can you make time for your professional development? Do your homework on the job (Microsoft's philosophy is that 70 percent of personal development takes place on the job, which aligns perfectly with the objectives of STCT). For example, if you have a fear of failure you need to find opportunities to work through the confidence trap. This may mean identifying moments where you can practice new ways of thinking and behaving, perhaps in a presentation or a meeting. Working through problems in real time is crucial to implementing the changes you need to effect in order to see positive results in your career.

Another way to create a 50-minute hour is to be more selfish. Selfishness gets a bad rap. It can be healthy and productive. Good selfishness is about putting yourself first but not at the expense of others. I have worked with many people who are physically and emotionally burned out from the effort it takes to be radiators at work and at home.

They need to redress their balance by finding time to invest in themselves. This doesn't have to mean they spend an hour a week navel gazing. A 50-minute hour can be spent doing an activity or pursuing an interest they find fulfilling. One woman I worked with had crashed and burned in her previous role and she was keen not to let it happen again. To redress the balance between work, home, and personal fulfillment she took up glassblowing as her mental health time. Another client went back to woodworking and, most interesting of all, one senior American vice president took up raising cows!

There is no doubt that for many of us work can be seductive. I have struggled with this problem in my own practice. The pace and energy, the constant challenge, and the feeling of making a difference can be intoxicating and exciting. The problem is that going full-force all the time is not sustainable and offers no opportunity to take time out for reflection or personal growth. That is why I have developed a support system to help me avoid getting crispy around the edges. You should, too.

Enlist Support

I often ask my clients to name the people who provide them with support and encouragement. The question often provokes a blank look and they often find the question difficult to answer. For some the dearth of support is a deliberate strategy. To them, enlisting the help of others equates with vulnerability. Others just never considered the possibility. Yet a successful outcome in STCT depends on enlisting the support of others. This support can take a several forms.

The expert. One resource leaders often ignore are other people in their organization, business, or team who excel at the very thing with which they are struggling. These may be individuals who exude self-confidence, have a clearly articulated set of beliefs, or use expert power to great effect. I ask my clients to observe, listen, and learn from these people, and if possible talk to them about how they managed to excel in these areas. Think about it. Who could you observe or shadow?

The trusted advisor. A further resource is people on your team who can act as your trusted advisors. One client was having significant problems running meetings so he asked two of his directs to give him feedback after every meeting. This way he was able to identify what was working and what wasn't. The feedback enabled him to reduce the size of his blind spot and accelerate his development.

Institutionalized feedback. I never, ever finish a meeting, whether with a team or one-on-one, without asking for feedback. This process has two purposes. The first is it that it helps make me more effective—I learn what is working and what isn't and what I need to do differently. The second is that it gives me a chance to role model asking for and receiving feedback. There are many ways you can incorporate feedback into your business. After a team meeting you can ask people to tell you how effective it was; if you want to increase your level of self-awareness you might want to ask, "What would you recommend I stop, start, or continue doing?" If you want to build trust you might manage expectations by asking, "What do you need from me to be successful?"

GHOSTS INTO ANCESTORS

The psychoanalyst Hans Loewald[3] explains that psychotherapy allows the "ghosts" of the past to be transformed into "ancestors" who positively impact thinking and behavior. I've seen how this can work firsthand. For example, as my business took off I sometimes felt the effects of the pressure to perform, and occasionally I became a little impatient, even harsh, with some of my more challenging patients. I was also beset by a recurring bad dream. In the dream I watched, with terror and amazement, a great white shark swim in the deep waters of the ocean. I spoke to my own analyst about the dream and he advised I find meaning in the dream and learn from it. I struggled to under-stand how a great white could teach me anything but not to get in the water. To help me, John shared the following story. One of his clients had been suffering from depression, but on one particular occasion came into his office in a much more positive frame of mind. He explained his sudden optimism by describing a dream. "I was swim-ming underwater surrounded by every type of exotic fish imaginable. Sunlight dappled the ocean bed and the water felt warm on my skin. I felt at peace in this idyllic setting. All of a sudden the fish darted away and the sun was replaced by shadow, and my feelings of peace were replaced by those of dread. Looking behind I saw a sea monster swim-ming toward me. Despite swimming as fast and as far as possible the monster gained ground. Finally I was trapped in an underwater canyon. The monster swam slowly toward me."

"What happened?" I interrupted, thinking of my own nightmare.

John replied, "He turned around and taught the monster how to sing."

I loved the story. What John was trying to tell me was that I needed to reframe the threat of the shark. Rather than the aggression and power of the great white haunting me, I needed to see it instead as an ancestor I could learn from and accept as part of myself. And eventu-ally that's what I did. One night I dreamed that I was entering a dark basement, with a window inset into the opposite wall. Through the window I could see the ocean. I approached it just as the shark swam up. This time, though, instead of cowering, I put my hand on the window and looked that shark straight in the eye.

I never had the dream again. I do realize, though, I have it in me to lose patience, be hypercritical, and threaten the very people I am trying to help. It's a side of myself I guard against but accept all the same, and there are times with some executives where the shark can come in very handy.

Over the years I have discovered that it is far better to teach our monsters (or ghosts, or sharks) to sing than to slay them, for they are part of us. They are our imperfections, and rather than ignore them we must recognize that they can provide important information about our past and present. I hope the lessons from this book will help you teach your own monster to sing.

Appendix

The Leadership Circumplex

The circumplex is based upon two related dimensions of leadership behavior—conviction and connection.

Conviction measures the following behaviors:

- The ability to provide a compelling *vision*;
- the capacity to manage or *lead change*;
- *reality sense*—the ability to grasp what is happening in the industry and a commitment to understanding and servicing the needs of the customer;
- the capacity to display *passion*, conviction, belief, and authenticity; and
- a commitment to continuous learning.

Connection measures the following:

- *Self-awareness*—an understanding of how your behavior affects others and how to change it according to the person/situation;
- *effective communication*—you demonstrate a sense of power and competence through communication;
- *developing people*—you put developing people as a priority and ensure that people have personal development plans; and
- the capacity to revitalize the business values.

However, the 360 provides much more than a summary of a leader's "conviction" or "connection"; it offers a multidimensional assessment of leadership capability and impact. The measures are described in detail below.

The Leadership Circumplex is illustrated on page 210. The following summary will help you interpret the model.

READING FROM THE INSIDE-OUT

The horizontal and vertical axes measure a person's level of conviction and connection, respectively. Higher scores—in combination—are better. For example, a a leader who scored 75 on conviction and 75 on connection would indicate high levels of each of these aspects.

The circumplex is divided into 4 quadrants—C1, C2, C3, and C4. Each provides a summary of a person's leadership style:

- *C1: High Conviction—Low Connection.* The C1 leader has a high level of conviction. He has vision and passion and is likely to lead from the front. Unfortunately, his people are likely to complain that they have no say in the direction of the business or of the goals or objectives they are working toward. This type of leader is likely to diminish, deny, or dismiss the important of relationships or partnerships. The C1 leader fails to balance his fierce drive to succeed with critical self-reflection and feedback. These people are often described as having "superior strategic skills" and "bandwidth" but the lack of "connection" skills can leave people "feel(ing) more like an "asset" which can be moved or redeployed at will, rather than an individual who needs to be motivated and enthused to be able to do my best work."

• *C2: High Conviction—High Connection.* The C2 leader has clarity of vision and a fierce will to succeed but she realizes that it is others who will get the "job" done. As such the C2 leader is assertive, confident, and can communicate her ideas effectively. Her people are better able to manage change as they realize what success looks like, and why the change is necessary. These people are usually described as "showing all the traits of a strong leader—strong people skills, vision, passion, great communication, and incredibly persuasive negotiators."

• *C3: Low Conviction—Low Connection.* The C3 leader has withdrawn from the leadership role. This may be a result of "burn out," a feeling that he has nothing more to give, or a failure to have impact and influence on the business—may result in a desire to remain "invisible"; and/or an inability to develop a strategic plan for the business, leaving people unsure of the purpose and direction of the team. Communication from the C3 leader will be sparse and uninspiring. He will fail to manage up effectively and the business may lose credibility and visibility and be inconsistent in decision making. Behavioral traits often exhibited by this type of leader include:

• *C4: Low Conviction—High Connection.* This leader tries to avoid conflict, and is often described as "diplomatic" in communications or negotiations with others. At its extreme, Type C4 leadership is driven more by the need for approval than making the tough decision. As such very few decisions are made and people are often confused as to the direction and purpose of the business. The C4 leader is often liked as a person, but disliked as someone to work for.

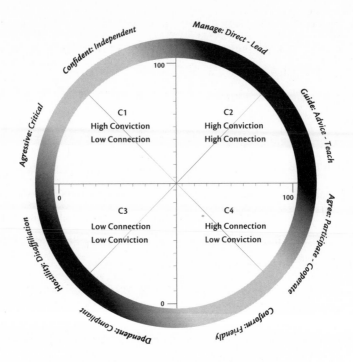

Leadership Transactions

The notations situated on the outside of the circle summarize eight distinct types of leadership behavior. These transactions describe both the behavioral characteristics of the leadership style and the likely effect it will have on others. Reading clockwise around the circumplex:

• *Manage: Direct—Lead.* This segment stresses leadership, energy, power, and expertise balanced with collaboration and support. Scores that fall in this area communicate the message I *am a strong, competent, knowledgeable person on whom you can rely for effective guidance and leadership.* This leader is likely to be very confident (both in her own capability and that of her team). She realizes that the team approach is one of the most effective ways of getting things done. This leadership style inspires respect, obedience, and support from others.

- *Guide: Advise—Teach.* The behaviors represented by this segment stress self-confidence and support. These leaders appear strong, but their power and confidence are used in a more affiliative way. They are more likely to use expert or referent power than rely on the authority inherent in their role. These people are often popular—they attempt to get along well with and to provoke respect from others. They have clear boundaries and, like the leader just described who directs and leads, are unlikely to compromise their beliefs or convictions in the face of conflict or disagreements. These leaders are good coaches and see developing their people as a key part of their role. This leadership style inspires respect and liking from others.

- *Agree: Participate—Cooperate.* These leaders are more likely to cooperate and compromise than direct and lead. The signature behaviors are conciliation and harmony. The motivation to be liked or approved of takes precedence over any expression of personal belief or conviction. The message communicated by this leadership style is *I am a friendly, agreeable nonthreatening person who would like you to like me.* As such they are less likely to emphasize a unique, original, or controversial point of view.

- *Conform: Friendly.* The conformist leader is driven by the need to fit in—with her team, the mores of the business, or the company culture. He or she will studiously avoid conflict, independence, or power. This person is most secure when she feels part of a team, and is most uncomfortable when called upon to make a decision or engage in any behavior which would make her visible and possibly out of step with the decisions of her team. She is more likely to respond by asking what others think than to express a clear view of her own.

- *Dependent: Compliant.* The dependent leader is predominantly passive. His signature behaviors include conformity, compliance,

211

suggestibility to the ideas of others, and high sensitivity to what others want or think. The dependent leader has low self-confidence and a passive interpersonal style. This leadership style is designed to encourage others to be protective, controlling, demanding, or nurturing.

- *Hostility: Dissatisfaction—Nonconformist.* These leaders avoid close, trusting relationships in favor of distrust, cynicism, and resentment. The purpose of this style is to challenge convention and maintain individuality; it provides a feeling of being different and unique. There are benefits to this style. It demands a healthy, critical approach to the accepted conventions, or the "way we do things around here." The biggest problem for people who work for the nonconformist is that he never *stands for anything* as he is *always against everything.* This style inspires anxious attachment.

- *Aggressive: Critical.* The keynote of this behavior is the expression of aggression. This may manifest itself as detachment and withdrawal, out-and-out confrontation, or passive-aggressive behavior. Signature behaviors include bluntness, criticism, cynicism, and distrust. These leaders are likely to ignore the needs, wants, opinions, feelings, or beliefs of others in favor of their own and constantly see any topic or idea as a contest of wills to win at all costs. These people are less interested in maintaining relationships than they are in being right. As such they are more likely to use role or coercive power to get things done than to rely on referent power or personal expertise. This style inspires fear, distrust, and anxiety.

- *Confident: Independent.* This segment returns to the more adaptive leadership themes outlined in the manage and guide segments—the difference being that in this case the guidance has a distinctly competitive component. At the extreme this leader might become narcissistic. I described the pros and cons of the narcissistic leader in chapter 3. These leaders can inspire and motivate or create chaos and hostility.

THE LEADERSHIP 360

The 42 items that make up the Leadership 360 are listed here. As you read through each of the behaviors decide how often you demonstrate each one—Rarely, Sometimes, Often, or Always. Be honest. If you like, checkpoint your assessments with others you work with. Also take the opportunity to write in the space provided your thoughts as to strengths or weaknesses in each of the nine areas.

Conviction

The following 5 dimensions describe the leader who demonstrates conviction.

1. Provides a guiding vision.

- Articulates a compelling vision of the future;
- expresses confidence that goals will be achieved;
- ensures that people in her business have a clear understanding of her expectations;
- instills faith, respect, and trust in her team; and
- communicates the steps required to achieve the vision.

Comments, observations, insight.

2. Manages change effectively.

- Is aware of the impact of change and ensures that everyone is aware of the implications for their role and responsibilities;
- builds a strong attachment to the team she leads;
- recognizes when it is time to change and when it is time to maintain stability; and
- is able to effectively manage resistance to change.

Comments, observations, insight.

3. Has a sense of reality.

- Has a firm grasp of what is happening in the industry and communicates this to her team;
- recognizes the importance of understanding and servicing the needs of the customer;
- believes that to perform effectively your business needs feedback from other parts of your company; and
- uses stories or shared experiences to help create a sense of attachment to her team.

Comments, observations, insight.

4. Displays passion.

- Displays conviction, belief, and authenticity in her role;
- people believe that working for you brings out the best in them;
- shows persistence and tenacity in the face of adversity or resistance; and
- is able to enthuse people with her passion and motivation.

Comments, observations, insight.

5. Promotes curiosity and learning.

- Provides opportunities to learn from successes and reflect on failures;

- facilitates learning on-the-job through feedback, listening, and questioning;
- Encourages people to think about problems in new ways
- forces people to reexamine critical assumptions; and
- promotes thinking, learning, and reflection as key business competencies.

Comments, observations, insight.

Connection

The following four dimensions describe the leader who demonstrates connection.

6. Is an effective communicator.

- Demonstrates a sense of power and competence through communication;
- does not avoid sensitive, confrontational, or difficult topics;
- is able to frame communication in a compelling fashion;
- is able to facilitate others in active and open dialogue;
- can give feedback constructively and in a nonjudgmental fashion; and
- carefully listens to what others have to say.

Comments, observations, insight.

```
┌─────────────────────────────────────────────────┐
│                                                 │
│                                                 │
│                                                 │
│                                                 │
│                                                 │
│                                                 │
│                                                 │
│                                                 │
│                                                 │
└─────────────────────────────────────────────────┘
```

7. Is self-aware.

- Actively seeks out feedback from different sources about her strengths and weaknesses;
- is aware of how her behavior affects others and changes it according to the person/situation; and
- can listen to feedback or criticism without becoming defensive, critical, or closed.

Comments, observations, insight.

```
┌─────────────────────────────────────────────────┐
│                                                 │
│                                                 │
│                                                 │
│                                                 │
│                                                 │
│                                                 │
│                                                 │
│                                                 │
│                                                 │
└─────────────────────────────────────────────────┘
```

8. Revitalizes the business values.

- Talks about her most important values and beliefs;
- lives these values on a daily basis;
- specifies the importance of having a strong sense of purpose;

- is willing to stand up for her ideas even if they are unpopular;
- follows through and keeps comitments; and
- considers the moral and ethical consequences of decisions she makes.

Comments, observations, insight.

```
┌─────────────────────────────────────────────┐
│                                             │
│                                             │
│                                             │
│                                             │
│                                             │
│                                             │
│                                             │
└─────────────────────────────────────────────┘
```

9. Developing people.

- Puts developing people as a priority and ensures that people have personal development plans;
- takes an interest in people;
- coaches, advises, and teaches people;
- understands that individuals have different needs, abilities, and aspirations; and
- is aware of people's development needs.

Comments, observations, insight.

```
┌─────────────────────────────────────────────┐
│                                             │
│                                             │
│                                             │
│                                             │
│                                             │
│                                             │
│                                             │
└─────────────────────────────────────────────┘
```

THE DEVELOPMENT BLUEPRINT

Creating your Blueprint

Research shows that your chances of achieving what is important to you go up 80 percent when you write down what you want to achieve and then check in periodically to monitor your progress. Creating a learning and development blueprint is a way for you to ensure your efforts are focused and purposeful. There are three stages to this process:

1. Identify what specific Leadership behaviors you want to focus on
2. Align your development needs with your business goals or objectives
3. Identify how you will create opportunities to learn on the "job"

Step 1 is the most important part of the whole process. When considering what behavior you want to change really focus on the drivers that lie beneath your actions. The net-net is look for the root cause of your behavior—don't build your blueprint around the symptoms.

Step 1: Identify

Key leadership behavior you want to focus on (identified from 360 and or discussions)	Problem to be solved (be specific—focus on the root cause not a symptom)	What will success look like 30 days from now? 60 days from now? 90 days from now?

Step 2: Linkage

Key leadership behavior you want to focus on (from previous table)	Your Business objectives (it's much easier to work on a specific behavior when it relates to a business goal or objective)	How will your development program help deliver your business objectives and goals?

Step 3: Synergy

The Microsoft philosophy is that 70 percent of learning and development should occur "on-the-job." Consequently the final stage in designing your "Blueprint" is to identify:

a.   What opportunities you have for development during your day-to-day activities. These may be many and varied: Meetings with your directs, 1:1's with your manager; presentations; cross-teaming, etc. Be creative—if opportunities don't exist—create them!!!

1.   Describe opportunity and how it will help your development goal

2.   Describe opportunity and how it will help your development goal

3.   Describe opportunity and how it will help your development goal

b.   The second area of learning in real time is to identify a person or persons who you feel demonstrates the very behavior you are trying to improve, who you can shadow or observe in action.
Name of person
How she/he can help

Name of person

How she/he can help

Step 4: Commitment to Continuous Learning

1. Are there any training courses you'd like to attend (short term or long term). How will they benefit your development?

Course

Benefit

Course

Benefit

Course

Benefit

2. Are there any experiences you'd like to have that could help you? What might these be? They could be a physical experience—climbing a mountain; an emotional experience—therapy perhaps; or a difficult conversation with a colleague, close friend or partner; or an intellectual experience.

Experience

Benefit

Experience

Benefit

Experience

Benefit

3. Are there any other resources you'd like to have available? For example, these might be books or tapes or an internal mentor.

Resource 1

Resource 2

Resource 3

Resource 4

Notes

1 FROM COUCH TO CORPORATE

1. The reasons for Freud's use of a couch are many and varied. My two favorites are that he wanted to thumb his nose at the conventions of the day and having a person, particularly a woman, recline in a man's office was definitely risqué for the times. The other was that Freud could not stand looking at his patients all the time so sitting behind a couch afforded him the opportunity to escape their gaze and look at the backs of their heads instead! J. A. Kottler, *On Being a Therapist* (San Francisco: Jossey-Bass, 2003), 287.

2. J. Gleick, *Faster* (New York: Pantheon Books, 1999), 324.

3. G. Harnois and P. Gabriel, "Mental Health at Work," in *Nations for Mental Health* (Geneva, Switzerland: World Health Organization, 2000), 77.

4. H. S. Sullivan, *The Interpersonal Theory of Psychiatry* (New York: W.W. Norton), 393.

5. J. A. C. Brown, *Freud and the Post-Freudian* (London: Penguin Books, 1972), 225.

6. N. Garmezy and M. Rutter, Eds., *Stress, Coping and Development in Children* (New York: McGraw Hill, 1983), 356.

7. S. Minuchin, *Families and Family Therapy* (Cambridge, MA: Harvard University Press, 1974), 268.

8. M. P. Nichols and R. C. Schwartz, *Family Therapy: Concepts and Methods*, 6th ed., P. Quinlin, ed. (Boston: Pearson, 2004), 489.

9. J. R. Katzenbach and D. K. Smith, *The Wisdom of Teams: Creating a High Performance Organization* (Boston: Harvard Business School Press, 1993), 291.

10. Nichols and Schwartz, *Family Therapy*, 489.

11. J. E. Groves, ed., *Essential Papers on Short-Term Dynamic Psychotherapy* (New York: New York University Press, 1996), 545.

12. S. D. Gosling and S. J. Ko, "A Room with a Cue: Personality Judgments Based on Offices and Bedrooms," *Journal of Personality and Social Psychology* 82, no. 3 (2002): 379–398.

13. Ibid.

14. Ibid.

15. T. Leary, *Interpersonal Diagnosis of Personality* (New York: The Ronald Press Company, 1957), 518.

16. L. K. Libby and R. Eibach, "Here's Looking at Me: The Effect of Memory Perspective on Assessment of Personal Change," *Journal of Personality and Social Psychology* 88, no. 1 (2005): 50–62.

17. S. H. Budman and A. S. Gurman, "Theory and Practice of Brief Therapy," in *Essential Papers on Short-Term Dynamic Therapy*, J. E. Groves, ed. (New York: New York University Press, 1996), 43–65.

18. M. Epstein, *Open to Desire: Embracing a Lust for Life* (New York: Gotham Books, 2005), 227.

2 BELIEF

1. S. Bedbury, *A New Brand World* (New York: Penguin, 2003), 220.

2. B. Levenson, *Bill Bernbach's Book: A History of Advertising that Changed the World* (New York: Villard, 1987), 220.

3. F. Walsh, "Beliefs, Spirituality, and Transcendence: Keys to Family Resilience," in *Re-Visioning Family Therapy*, M. McGoldrick, ed. (The Guilford Press: New York, 1998), 62–77.

4. R. Branson, *Losing My Virginity: How I've Survived, Had Fun, and Made a Fortune Doing Business My Way* (New York: Crown Business, 1999), 370.

5. J. Wheeler, "Are You Experienced? Why the Customer Experience is now Top of the CEO's Agenda," *Directorship*, March 2003.

6. S. Lohr, "Preaching from the Ballmer Pulpit," *New York Times*, Business Section, January 28, 2007.

7. Lohr, "Preaching from the Bullmer Pulpit."

8. B. McLean and P. Elkind, *The Smartest Guys in the Room: The Amazing Rise and Scandalous Fall of Enron* (New York: Penguin Books, 2004), 440.

9. L. Fox, *Enron: The Rise and Fall* (Hoboken NJ: Wiley, 2003), 189.

10. J.C. Collins and J. I. Portis, *Built to Last: Successful Habits of Visionary Companies* (New York: Harper Business Essentials, 2002), 342.

11. Collins Portis, *Built to Last*, 342.

12. P. Montoya, *A Brand Called You* (Tustin: Peter Montoya Publishers, 2002), 278.

13. Y. Chouinard, *Let My People Go Surfing: The Education of a Reluctant Businessman* (New York: Penguin, 2005), 260.

14. Levenson, *Bill Bernbach's Book*, 220.

15. Levenson, *Bill Bernbach's Book*, 220.

16. DDB, "Our Heritage," http://www.ddbconnect.com/sitemap.

17. T. H. Holmes and R. H. Rahe, "The Social Readjustment Scale," *Journal of Psychomatic Research* 11 (1967): 213–218.

18. I. M. Goodyer, C. Wright, and P. M. E. Altham, "Maternal Adversity and Recent Stressful Life Events in Anxious and Depressed Children, *Journal of Child Psychology and Psychiatry* 29 (1988), 651–667.

19. N. Garmezy, "Stressors of Childhood," in *Stress, Coping and Development in Children*, N. Garmezy and M. Rutter, eds. (New York: McGraw-Hill, 1983), 43–84.

20. W. H. Bovey and A. Hede, "Resistance to Organizational Change: The Role of Defense Mechanisms," *Journal of Managerial Psychology* 16, no. 7 (2001): 534–548.

21. S. Jobs, "You've Got to Find What You Love," *Stanford Report 2005* [cited June 14].

22. H. Schultz and D. J. Yang, *Pour Your Heart into It: How Starbucks Built a Company One Cup at a Time* (New York: Hyperion, 1997), 351.

23. B. Bettelheim, *The Uses of Enchantment: The Meanings and Importance of Fairy Tales* (New York: Vintage, 1989), 328.

24. S. Denning, "Telling Tales," *Harvard Business Review* (May 2004): 9.

25. H. Gardner, *Leading Minds: Anatomy of Leadership* (New York: Basic Books, 1995), 400.

26. H. Ibarra and K. Lineback, "What's Your Story," *Harvard Business Review* (January 2005): 7.

27. S. Denning, "Telling Tales," *Harvard Business Review* (May 2004): 9.

28. S. Jobs, "You've Got to Find What You Love," *Stanford Report 2005* [cited June 14].

29. W. P. Rogers, "Report of the PRESIDENTIAL COMMISSION on the Space Shuttle Challenger Accident," Washington, D.C., 1986, 225.

30. Columbia Accident Investigation Board, *Columbia Accident Investigation Report* (Washington, D.C.: Government Printing Office, 2003), 99–117.

31. *Columbia Accident Investigation Report*, 99–117.

32. "Report of the PRESIDENTIAL COMMISSION on the Space Shuttle Challenger Accident," 225.

33. F. Walsh, "Religion and Spirituality: Wellsprings for Healing and Resilience," in *Spiritual Resources in Family Therapy*, F. Walsh, ed. (New York: The Guilford Press, 1999), 301.

34. D. K. Osbon, ed. *Reflections on the Art of Living: A Joseph Campbell Companion* (New York: HarperPerennial, 1991), 311.

3 CONFIDENCE

1. D. D. Burns, *Feeling Good: The New Mood Therapy* (New York: New American Library, 1980), 416.

2. R. M. Kanter, *Confidence: How Winning Streaks and Losing Streaks Begin and End* (New York: Three Rivers Press, 2006), 432.

3. Formula adapted from "Confidence" by Carol Craig, Centre for Confidence and Wellbeing, 2006.

4. H. S. Sullivan, *The Interpersonal Theory of Psychiatry* (New York: W.W. Norton, 1953), 393.

5. Information on "Rock of Gibraltar," http://en.wikipedia.org/wiki/Rock_of_ gibraltar.

6. Burns, *New Mood Therapy*.

7. Excerpted from Mark Binelli, "The Most Honest Man in News," *Rolling Stone*, March 2007.

8. J. O. Cavenar and D. S. Werman, "Origins of the Fear of Success," *American Journal of Psychiatry* 13, no. 1 (1981): 95–98.

9. A further cause is the guilt some women feel on achieving more than their parents or co-workers. This is less a confidence issue than a self-esteem issue. Women often report feeling bad about themselves because they are successful and others have not been. Men rarely struggle with this type of guilt.

10. R. M. Gilbert, *Extraordinary Relationships: A New Way of Thinking About Human Interactions* (Minneapolis: Chronimed Publishing, 1992).

11. D. W. Winnicott, *Playing and Reality* (London: Penguin, 1980), 194.

12. P. Clance, *The Imposter Phenomenon: Overcoming the Fear that Haunts Your Success* (Peachtree Publishers Ltd., 1989).

13. B. Lask and A. Fosson, *Childhood Illness: The Psychosomatic Approach: Children Talking With Their Bodies.* Wiley Series in Family Psychology (Chichester: John Wiley & Sons, 1989), 174.

14. In *Perfectionism: Theory, Research and Treatment*, G. Flett and P. Hewitt, eds. (American Psychological Association, 2000).

15. C. Foster, *The Family Patterns Workbook* (New York: Putnam, 1993), 235.

16. M. McKay and P. Fanning, *Self-Esteem: A Proven Program of Cognitive Techniques for Assessing, Improving, and Maintaining Your Self-Esteem* (New Harbinger Publications, 2000), 316.

17. A. Hertzfeld, *Reality Distortion Field*, February 1981.

18. M. Wilson, *The Difference Between God and Larry Ellison* (New York: Harper Business, 1997), 399.

19. M. F. Solomon, *Narcissism and Intimacy* (New York: W. W. Norton, 1992), 217.

20. W. K. Campbell, A. S. Goode, and J. D. Foster, "Narcissism, Confidence, and Risk Attitude," *Journal of Behavioral Decision Making* 17 (2004): 297–311.

21. M. Maccoby, "Narcissistic Leaders: The Incredible Pros, the Inevitable Cons," *Harvard Business Review*, 2004.

22. E. Hatfield, J. T. Cacioppo, and R. L. Rapson, "Emotional Contagion," *Studies in Emotion & Social Interaction* (Paris: Cambridge University Press, 1994), 241.

23. K. R. Jamison, *Exuberance: The Passion for Life* (New York: Vintage, 2005), 405.

24. This article appeared in *Newsweek*, August 8, 1988, and was cited in *Emotional Contagion*, Hatfield et al. (1994), 177.

25. J. Nocera, "Fewer Eggs and More Baskets in the Incubator," *New York Times*, 2006.

26. R. Solnit, *Hope in the Dark: The Untold History of People Power* (Edinburgh: Canongate, 2004), 170.

27. R. Branson, *Losing My Virginity: How I've Survived, Had Fun, and Made a Fortune Doing Business My Way* (New York: Crown Business, 1999), 370.

4 SELF-AWARENESS AND YOUR BEHAVIORAL SIGNATURE

1. W. Bennis, *On Becoming a Leader* (New York: Basic, 2003), 218.

2. J. Luft, *Of Human Interaction*, 5th ed. (Palo Alto: National Press, 1969), 177.

3. B. Turvey, *Criminal Profiling: An Introduction to Behavioral Evidence Analysis*, 2nd ed. (San Diego: Academic Press, 2002), 717.

4. K. Back and K. Back, *Assertiveness at Work: A Practical Guide to Handling Awkward Situations*, 2nd ed. (London: McGraw Hill International, 1991), 166.

5. R. F. Rakos, "Assertive Behavior: Theory, Research and Training," in *International Series on Communication Skills*, O. Hargie, ed. (London: Routledge, 1991), 248.

6. R. G. Ryder and S. Bartle, "Boundaries as Distance Regulators in Personal Relationships," *Family Process* 30 (1991): 393–406.

7. B. Wood, and M. Talmon, "Family Boundaries in Transition: A Search for Alternatives," *Family Process* 22 (1983): 2, 347–357.

8. S. Minuchin, *Families and Family Therapy* (Cambridge, MA: Harvard University Press, 1974), 268.

9. W. Oncken and D. L. Wass, "Management Time: Who's Got the Monkey," *Harvard Business Review*, November–December 1999.

10. J. Bowlby, *A Secure Base. Clinical Implications of Attachment Theory* (London: Routledge, 1992), 180.

11. J. Feeney and P. Noller, *Adult Attachment*. Sage Series on Close Relationships (London: Sage, 1996), 176.

12. C. Hazan and P. R. Shaver, "Love and Work: An Attachment—Theoretical," *Journal of Personality and Social Psychology* 59, no. 2 (1990): 270–280.

13. C. Hazan and P. Shaver, "Romantic Love Conceptualized as an Attachment Process," *Journal of Personality and Social Psychology* 52 (1987): 511–524.

14. J.-E. Dimitrius and M. Mazzarella, *Reading People: How to Understand People and Predict their Behavior Anytime, Anyplace* (New York: Random House, 1998), 281.

15. S. Baron-Cohen, *Mindblindness: An Essay on Autism and Theory of Mind* (Massachusetts: MIT Press, 1997), 171.

16. P. Ekman, "Facial Expressions," in *Handbook of Cognition and Emotion*, T. Dalgleish and M. Power, eds. (Hoboken: Wiley, 1999).

17. P. Ekman, "Darwin, Deception, and Facial Expression," *Annals of the New York Academy of Science* (2003): 205–221.

18. Ekman has spent his career studying the psychology of facial expression and I have found his writing and instructional CDs to be very useful in my practice.

19. P. Ekman, "Facial Expressions and Emotion," *American Psychologist* 48, no. 4 (1993): 348–392.

20. J. Syer and C. Connolly, *The Self Awareness Continuum* (London: 1992).

5 TRUST

1. F. Fukuyama, *Trust* (New York: Free Press, 1995), 480.

2. Yankelovich, *National Leadership Index 2005: A National Study of Confidence in Leadership* (Harvard: Harvard University, 2005), 18.

3. W. E. Forum, *Trust In Governments, Corporations and Global Institutions Continues to Decline*. Volume 5, 2005.

4. R. Galford and A. S. Drapeau, "The Enemies of Trust," *Harvard Business Review* (2003).

5. R. M. Kramer, "Trust and Distrust in Organizations: Emerging Perspectives, Enduring Questions," *Annual Review of Psychology* (1999).

6. R. Galford and A. Drapeau, "The Enemies of Trust," *Harvard Business Review*, February 2003.

7. M. Yuki, et al., "Cross-Cultural Differences in Relationship and Group Based Trust," *Society for Personality and Social Psychology* 31, no. 1 (2005): 48–62.

8. C. Handy, "Trust and the Virtual Organization," *Harvard Business Review* (May–June 1995).

9. *The Economist* (December 16, 1995): 16.

10. Ibid.

11. J. Deal, K. S. Wampler, and C. F. Halverson, "The Importance of Similarity in the Marital Relationships," *Family Process* 31 (1992): 369–382.

12. D. Consulting, *A DDI Study in Leadership Transitions: Stepping Up, Not Off* (2007).

13. M. E. Kerr and M. Bowen, *Family Evaluation: An Approach Based on Bowen Theory* (New York: Norton, 1988).

6 POWER AND AMBITION

1. R. A. Caro, "Lessons in Power: Lyndon Johnson Revealed," *Harvard Business Review*, 2006.

2. S. Milgram, "Behavioral Study of Obedience," *Journal of Abnormal and Social Psychology* 67, no. 4 (1963): 371–378.

3. J. N. Nye, *Soft Power: The Means to Success in World Politics* (New York: Public Affairs, 2004), 191.

4. L. Gray, *Power: How its Meaning in Corporate Life is Changing*. Harvard Management Update, 1996.

5. E. S. Person, *Feeling Strong: How Power Issues Affect our Ability to Direct Our Own Lives* (New York: Harper Collins, 1972).

6. J. R. French and B. Raven, "The Bases of Social Power," in *Studies in Social Power*, D. Cartwright, ed. (Ann Arbor, MI: University of Michigan, 1959), 225.

7. M. Buchanan, *Nexus: Small Worlds and the Groundbreaking Theory of Networks* (New York: Norton, 2002), 235.

8. J. Freeman, "Emotional Problems of the Gifted Child," *Journal of Child Psychology and Psychiatry* 24 (1983): 481–485.

9. D. K. Osbon, ed. *Reflections on the Art of Living: A Joseph Campbell Companion* (New York: HarperPerennial, 1991), 311.

10. *Diagnostic and Statistical Manual of Mental Disorders: DSM-IV-TR*, Fourth Edition (American Psychiatric Press, 2000).

7 BE YOUR OWN THERAPIST

1. E. S. Person, *Feeling Strong: How Power Issues Affect our Ability to Direct Our Own Lives* (New York: HarperCollins, 2002).

2. G. E. Vaillant, "Mental Health. 2003," *American Journal of Psychiatry* (August 2003): 1373–1384.

3. G. Lewis, "From Ghosts to Ancestors: The Psychoanalytic Vision of Hans Loewald," *American Journal of Psychoanalysis* 58, no. 3 (1998): 337–338.

Index